LAROUSSE

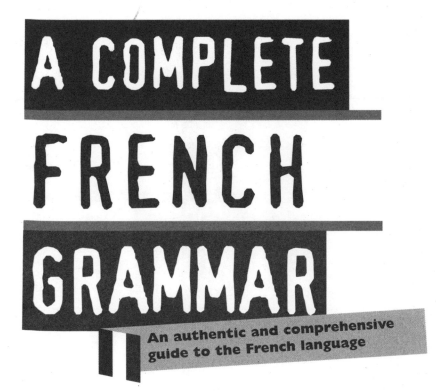

A COMPLETE FRENCH GRAMMAR

An authentic and comprehensive guide to the French language

LAROUSSE

English version
Victor HARGREAVES
John GIBSON

Review of text
Robert DAVREU
Françoise DAVREU

Typesetting
Josiane SAYAPHOUM

Editor
Clémence CORNU
Charlotte DAVREU

SUMMARY

PART III : FROM THE PHRASE TO THE TEXT

APPENDICE

ALPHABETICAL INDEX

PART I
INTRODUCTION

ORIGINS OF THE FRENCH LANGUAGE

The French language was born out of the Latin that the Roman conquerers introduced into Gaul during the 1st century BC. This spoken Latin, which was very different from literary Latin, replaced the language of the Gauls. Only some place names (*Paris, Chartres, etc.*) and words to do with country life (*arpent*/acre, *borne*/boundary stone, *charrue*/plough, etc.) remind us today of the Gaulish language of the past.

POPULAR WORD FORMATION AND LEARNED WORD FORMATION

Latin words, through changes in their pronunciation and developments from their original meaning, have become, over time, French words (popular word formation). However, since the beginning of the Middle Ages, scholars have created other words, basing them directly on Latin words (learned word formation). Thus:

> the Latin word *locare* evolved into *louer*/to rent (popular word formation);

> the word *location*/rental has been created directly from the Latin *locatio* (learned word formation).

Furthermore, the same Latin word has sometimes been responsible for two words in modern French. The two words with the same origin are known as a doublet:

> *auscultare* has given *écouter*/to listen (popular word formation) and *ausculter*/to sound the chest of (learned word formation).

DEVELOPMENT OF THE FRENCH LANGUAGE

During the Middle Ages, the early French language (known as "Romance"), evolved in different ways in the different regions of France; the "langue d'oïl" in the north, the "langue d'oc" in the south, and the "francien" dialect in the region of Paris.

It was "francien", the language of the Capetian kings, which became the national language, reducing the other languages (notably Champenois, Picard, and Norman) to the status of dialects or local speech.

Thus "francien" became the French language, and spread out over the Royal domaine to take on the role of a national language. Today other languages still exist in France alongside French: Breton, Basque, Alsatian, Flemish, Provençal and Langue d'oc.

Some variations have appeared between the French spoken in France and the French spoken in other parts of the French speaking world, and these have led to characteristics which are easily noticeable in one country or another. They are mostly found in the spoken language and in the choice of words (vocabulary).

PRONUNCIATION

The different ways of pronouncing the same word has created phonetic variations which characterise the different regions of the French speaking world:

un is pronounced [ɛ̃] in Paris;

un is pronounced [œ̃] in Montreal and in Rennes (regional capital of Britanny).

We can thus identify according to their pronunciation a Parisian, a person from Montreal, a Belgian, and a person from Geneva or from Marseilles.

VOCABULARY

The main differences between the French of different regions are often noticed in the choice of vocabulary. Each French region or French speaking country has particular characteristics (flora and fauna, geography, cultural aspects, attitudes of mind, etc.) and these have given rise to particular lexical items:
– Belgian: *aubrette*/bus shelter...
– Swiss: *raclette*/raclette, *votation*/voting...
– Canadian/Quebeker: *motoneige*/snowcat, *cégep*/secondary school, *téléroman*/TV serial...
– African: *boubou*/loose garment, *marabout*/marabout stork...
These modern regional variations are often mentioned in dictionaries published in France. They contribute to the development and enrichment of the French language.

FOREIGN LOAN WORDS

The everyday vocabulary of modern French is more than 80 % of Latin origin, either through popular or learned word formation. The remainder comes from the languages of civilisations with which France and the French people have been in contact. When new words come from a foreign language they are known as "loan words".
Over the years the French language has borrowed words from a number of foreign languages:
– *guerre*/war, *bannière*/banner come from Germanic languages;
– *vague*/wave, *varech*/kelp are of Scandanavian origin;
– *banque, carnaval* come from Italian;
– *fiesta*/holiday, *tabac*/tobacco are from Spanish;
– *choucroute, kitsch* come from German;
– *matelot*/sailor, *cambuse*/storeroom are from Dutch;
– *algèbre*/algebra, *alcool*/alcohol come from Arabic;

– *jazz, film* come from English;
– *café, thé* come from the East;
– *canot/*canoe, *cacao/*cocoa are from Amerindian languages.

A number of these loan words have not entered French directly; Italian, English, Spanish, Portuguese have served as intermediaries for many of the words used today: for example, *café* comes from the Italian caffè, itself borrowed from the Arabic *qhwa*, pronounced "kahvé" in Turkish.
At the present time, most of the loan words come from English, and mainly from American English (ex: *jeans*). This important influence comes from the dominance of American civilisation in a number of areas: science and technology, mass culture, media and sport. Some of these loan words reflect passing fashions and are often only temporary (ex: *dandy, beatnik)*. Other words are permanent loan words which have become incorporated into the French language, either unchanged (ex: *design, gadget)* or adapted and integrated (ex: *attaché-case, faisabilité, camping)*.
Borrowings from other languages are not so common, but we can mention a few examples: *pizzeria* (Italian), *karatéka* (Japanese), *macho* (Spanish), *ersatz* (German), *goulag* (Russian), *diaspora* (Greek), etc.

New WORDS

New words are continually being formed in order to reflect developments in society and to meet the needs of scientific progress. These words are created in different ways and are often the same in many languages. These new words are known as "neologisms" or nonce words.

WORDS OF GREEK ORIGIN

In order to form new words, word borrowings are often made from the Greek language. For example:
– **télé** meaning "far away" or "from far", has been used to create:

télégramme, téléphone, télémètre, téléobjectif, télévision, télépathie, téléscope, télécommunication, téléski, téléguidage, etc.;

– **graphein** means "writing" or "describing" and has been used to create the following words:

calligraphie, sténographie, biographie, géographie, topographie, cosmographie, photographie, graphologie, radiographie, graphomètre, graphisme, graphique, télégraphique, etc.

DERIVATION AND COMPOUNDING

A language develops by forming derived words and compound words. By adding an ending, called a suffix, to a single word, a derived word can be formed.
Thus, in *journalisme*/journalism, the suffix **-isme** is added to the word *journal*/newspaper, to form a derived word. This process is known as "derivation".

Journal appeared in the 12th century;
journalisme in the 17th century.

A compound word can often be formed by preceding a single word by a syllable or group of syllables known as a prefix. In *préjuger*/to prejudge, the prefix **pré-** is put at the beginning of the word *juger*/to judge to form a compound word. This process is known as "compounding".

Juger appeared in the 12th century; *préjuger* in the 16th century.

▉COMPOUND WORDS WITH MORE THAN ONE ELEMENT

Language forms a large number of new words by joining up two or more words (noun + noun, adjective + noun, verb + noun, etc.). Strictly speaking, these are the real compound words.

chou-fleur/cauliflower, *plate-bande*/flower bed, *arrière-garde*/rearguard, *garde-malade*/nurse.

Usually a hyphen is placed between the different elements of these words, but some compound words do not take a hyphen (*pomme de terre*/potato) and others are written as single words (*gentilhomme*/ gentleman).

WORD FAMILIES AND LEXICAL FIELD

A word family is a group of compound and derived words formed from the same single word, known as the "radical", and which make up a lexical field, meaning a group of words related both through meaning and form. For example, for the word family "classe", we have:

– derived words: *classeur, classer, classique, classicisme, classifier, classification, classement*;
– compound words, adding a prefix to the word "classe" or its derivatives: *déclasser, déclassement, surclasser, surclassement, reclasser, reclassement, interclasse*;
– proper compound words incorporating one or more terms: *hors classe*/classless, *sous-classe*/underclass.

SUFFIXES

Suffixes, which are numerous and of different origin, often have precise meaning. Thus, **-et, -ot, -cule, -ille**, have a diminutive function and indicate something small:

> garçon**net**/small boy, îl**ot**/small island, animal**cule**/animalcule, fauc**ille**/sickle, brind**ille**/twig, flot**ille**/flotilla.

Others may have several meanings, sometimes quite vague; for example, the suffix **-erie** indicates the place where a particular trade is carried on:

> épic**erie**/grocery, sucr**erie**/sugar refinery, fond**erie**/foundry, tuil**erie**/tilery, boulang**erie**/bakery.

But it can also indicate the manner of being or the general ensemble:

> la gris**erie**/intoxication, la fourb**erie**/treachery, l'argent**erie**/silverware.

Suffixes can be added directly to single words, but the final silent **-e** of a single word disappears before a vowel, and consonants are sometimes inserted between the suffix and the single word:

> serrure → serrur**ier**/locksmith
> pigeon → pigeon-**n-eau**/young pigeon
> bijou → bijou-**t-ière**/jeweller

Suffixes can be:

● suffixes proper, that is to say elements made up of one or more syllables (**-able, -ier, -erie, -tion, -oir, -té, -ment**, etc.):

> insépar**able**/inseparable, journal**ier**/daily, bois**erie**/panelling, posi**tion**/position, arros**oir**/watering can, clar**té**/light, panse**ment**/dressing;

● words of Greek or Latin origin used as suffixes; for example:
– in the word *viticulture*, there are two elements: **viti-** (from the Latin *vitis*, a vine), and **-culture**; this last word has the role of a suffix;
– in *hydrogène*/hydrogen, there are two elements: **hydro-** (from the Greek *hudor*, water) and **-gène** (from a Greek word meaning "which creates"); this last element has the role of a suffix.
Suffixes often differ according to whether they are used to form nouns, adjectives, verbs or adverbs.

PROPER SUFFIXES

■ Suffixes used to form nouns

Suffix	Meaning	Examples	Suffix	Meaning	Examples
-ace	pejorative	*populace*	-esse	quality, lack	*sagesse*
-asse		*filasse*			*maladresse*
-ade	action, collective	*orangeade*	-et, -ette	diminutive	*garçonnet*
-age	action, collective	*balayage*			*fillette*
-aie	plantation	*cerisaie*	-été	quality, lack	*propreté*
-ail	instrument	*éventail*			*méchanceté*
-aille	pejorative, collective	*ferraille*	-eur	agent	*rôdeur*
-ain	origin	*Romain*	-euse		*acheteuse*
-en		*Vendéen*	-ie	state	*jalousie*
-aine	collective	*dizaine*	-ien	profession	*chirugien*
-aire	agent	*incendiaire*	-enne		*musicienne*
-ance	result of action	*croyance*	-illon	diminutive	*aiguillon*
-ence		*virulence*	-is	result of action,	*ramassis*
-ard	pejorative	*chauffard*		state	
-at	profession, status	*internat*	-ise	quality, lack of	*franchise*
-(a)teur	agent, trade	*dessinateur*			*sottise*
-trice		*institutrice*	-isme	doctrine	*idéalisme*
-tion	action	*fabrication*	-iste	profession	*dentiste*
-sion		*omission*	-iste	specialist	*chauffagiste*
		exclusion		follower	*socialiste*
-aison		*livraison*	-ite	illness	*gastrite*
-âtre	pejorative	*marâtre*	-ité,-té	quality	*cherté*
-(a)ture	action,	*peinture*	-itude	quality, state	*exactitude*
	instrument	*armature*			*servitude*
-aud	pejorative	*maraud*	-ment	action, state	*bêlement*
-cule,-ule	diminutive	*globule*			*tassement*
-eau	diminutive	*chevreau*	-oir	instrument	*perchoir*
-elle		*radicelle*	-oire	instrument	*baignoire*
-ée	contents	*assiettée*	-ole	diminutive	*bestiole*
-er/-ère	agent, trade	*boucher*	-on	diminutive	*ourson*
-ier/-ière		*pâtissière*	-eron		*moucheron*
-erie	quality, lack of	*galanterie*	-on	scientific	*neutron*
-erie	premises	*charcuterie*	-ot	diminutive	*îlot*
			-ille		*brindille*

■ Suffixes used to form adjectives

Suffix	Meaning	Examples	Suffix	Meaning	Examples
-able, -ble	possibility	aimable, audible	-et, -elet	diminutive	propret, aigrelet
-ain, -ien	occupier	africain, indien	-eux	derived noun	peureux,
-ais	origin	japonais,			valeureux
-ois, -an		chinois, birman	-iel	which belongs	concurrentiel
-aire	which belongs	solaire, polaire	-ier	quality	hospitalier, altier
-al	quality	vital, glacial	-if	quality	oisif, maladif
-asse, -ard	pejorative	fadasse, faiblard	-in	diminutive	blondin, plaisantin
-âtre	diminutive	bleuâtre		& pejorative	
	& pejorative	douceâtre	-ique	relative to	chimique, ironique
-aud	pejorative	lourdaud, rustaud	-iste	relative to	réaliste, égoïste
-é	state	bosselé, dentelé	-ot	diminutive	pâlot, vieillot
-el	which causes	accidentel, mortel		& pejorative	
-esque	quality	romanesque,	-u	quality	barbu, charnu
		dantesque			

■ Suffixes used to form verbs

Suffix	Meaning	Examples	Suffix	Meaning	Examples
-ailler	pejorative	tournailler	-iner	diminutive	piétiner
-asser	pejorative	rêvasser	-ir	derived adj.	verdir
-eler	derived noun	marteler	-iser	make become	angliciser
-er	derived noun	vacciner	-ocher	pejorative	effilocher
-eter	diminutive	tacheter	-onner	pejorative	chantonner
-ifier	make become	solidifier	-oter	pejorative	toussoter
-iller	diminutive	mordiller	-oyer	become	poudroyer

■ Suffixes used to form adverbs

Suffix	Meaning	Examples	Suffix	Meaning	Examples
-ment	manner	gentiment	-ons	manner	à reculons

▬LATIN AND GREEK ELEMENTS USED AS SUFFIXES

■ Suffixes based on Latin words

Suffix	Meaning	Examples	Suffix	Meaning	Examples
-cide	which kills	insecticide	-fuge	who or which flees	transfuge,
-cole	related to culture	agricole		from	fébrifuge
-cole	which lives in	arboricole	-grade	who or which walks	plantigrade
-culteur	who cultivates	motoculteur	-lingue	language	bilingue
-culture	cultivation	apiculture	-pare	who or which	ovipare
-fère	which carries	mammifère		gives birth	
-fère	which contains	crucifère	-pède	who or which has	bipède
-fique	which produces	frigorifique		feet	
-forme	in form of	cunéiforme	-vore	who or which	carnivore
				feeds on	

■ Suffixes based on Greek words

Suffix	Meaning	Examples	Suffix	Meaning	Examples
-algie	pain	névralgie	-morphe	form	anthropomorphe
-arche	who orders	patriache	-nome	who or which rules	économe
-arque		monarque			
-archie	commanding	anarchie	-nomie	art of ruling	autonomie
-bar(e)	pressure	millibar, isobare	-onyme	name	patronyme
-bole	who or which throws	discobole	-pathe	sick with	névropathe
			-pathie	strong feeling, illness	sympathie
-carpe	fruit	péricarpe			myopathie
-céphale	head	encéphale	-pédie	education	encyclopédie
-crate	who manages	démocrate	-phage	who eats	anthrophage
-cratie	power	ploutocratie	-phagie	act of eating	hippophagie
-cycle	wheel	tricycle	-phile	friend of	russophile
-game	which unites	bigame	-philie	friendship for	francophilie
-gamie	marriage	bigamie	-phobe	enemy of	anglophobe
-gène	which generates	pathogène	-phobie	fear of	agoraphobie
			-phone	sound, speech	francophone
-gramme	written	télégramme	-phonie	sound	radiophone
-graphe	which writes	biographe	-phore	which carries	sémaphore
-graphie	art of writing, of describing	calligraphie, géographie	-pode	foot	gastéropode
			-ptère	wing	hélicoptère
-hydre	water	anhydre	-scope	which sees	téléscope
-id(e)	which has the form of	sinusoïde	-scopie	vision	radioscopie
			-sphère	a sphere	stratosphère
-lâtrie	adoration	idolâtrie	-technie	science	électrotechnie
-lithe	stone	monolithe	-technique	which knows	polytechnique
-logie	science	astrologie	-thèque	cupboard	bibliothèque
-logue	who studies	neurologue	-thérapie	healing	héliothérapie
-mancie	tell the future	cartomancie	-tome	which cuts	atome
-mane	enthralled	opiomane	-tomie	action of cutting	trachéotomie
		mélomane	-type	printing	Linotype
-manie	mania for	anglomanie	-type	model	prototype
-mètre	measure	centimètre	-typie	which prints	linotypie

PREFIXES

Prefixes, of Greek or Latin origin, are put at the beginning of a word, but certain changes sometimes take place when they are in contact with the initial consonant of a single word:

in- indicates the lack of → *in-actif* /inactive; but *im-patient*/impatient, *ir-réalisable*/unachievable, *il-logique*/illogical

We distinguish between:

• proper prefixes:

circum- (= around); **ex-** (= out of), etc.;

• words of Greek or Latin origin taking the role of components used as prefixes:

in *bioéthique*, *biosphère*, etc., **bio-** (from the Greek *bios*, "life") is a prefix.

■ Prefixes of Latin origin

Prefix	Meaning	Examples	Prefix	Meaning	Examples
ab-,	far from	abduction	juxta-	near to	juxtaposer
abs-		abstinence	male-	evil	malédiction
ad-	towards	adjoint	mau-	evil	maudire
ambi-	two	ambidextre	pén(é)	almost	pénéplaine
anté-	before	antédiluvien	per-, par-	across	perforer, parcourir
anti-	before	antichambre	post-	after	postdater
bis-, bi-	two	biscuit, bipède	pré-	before	précéder
circon-	around	circonvolution	pro-	forward	projeter
circum-	around	circumnavigation	pour-	in front of	pourtour
co-,	with	coadjuteur	quasi-	almost	quasi-délit
col-,		collaborateur	ré-, r(e)-	again	réargenter
com-,		commandant	rétro-	backwards	rétroviseur
cor-		corrélatif	simili-	similar	similigravure
dis-,	separate	dissymétrie	sub-,	under	subalterne
		disjoncteur	sous-,		sous-location
dé-, des-,		désunion	suc-		succomber
di-		digression	super-,	above	superstructure
entre-	between	entresol	sur-		surhomme
ex-	outside of	expatrier	supra		supranational
é-, ex-	deprived of	édenté, exfolié	trans-,	beyond	transhumant
extra-	very	extrafin	tré-		trépasser
extra-	out of	extraordinaire	tres-	across	tressaillement
il-, im-,	deprived of	illettré, imberbe	tri-,	three	tripartite
in-, ir-		indécent, irrespect	tris-		trisaïeul
in-, im-	in	infiltrer, importer	ultra-,	beyond	ultraviolet
inter-	between	international	outre-		outre-mer
intra-	within	intraveineux	vice-, vi-	in place of	vice-consul, vicomte

■ Prefixes of Greek origin

Prefix	Meaning	Examples	Prefix	Meaning	Examples
a-, an-	without	amoral, anarchie	épi-	on, towards	épiderme
amphi-	around	amphithéâtre	eu-	well	euphonie
	double	amphibie	exo-	outside	exotique
anti-	against	antialcoolique	hémi-	half	hémisphère
apo-	far from	apogée	hyper-	above	hypertrophie
arch(i)-	to highest degree	archifou	hypo-	under	hypoténuse
cata-	high to low	cataracte	méta-	change, after	métamorphose, métacarpe
di(a)-	across, separated from	diaphane, diagonal	par(a)-	against	parallèle
dys-	with difficulty	dyspepsie	péri-	around	périmètre
en-	in	encéphale	pro-	for, in front	programme
end(o)-	within	endocrine	syn-,	with	syndicat
			sym-		sympathie

■ Prefixes based on Latin words

Prefix	Meaning	Examples	Prefix	Meaning	Examples
acét(o)-	vinager	*acétate*	multi-	numerous	*multiforme*
aqu(i)-	water	*aqueduc*	octa-,	eight	*octaèdre*
arbor-	tree	*arboriculture*	octo-		*octosyllable*
calc-	chalk	*calcaire*	omni-	all	*omnivore*
calor-	heat	*calorifère*	pluri-	several	*pluriannuel*
carbo-	coal	*carbochimie*	prim(i)-	first	*primordial*
carn-	flesh	*carnivore*	quadr(i)-	four	*quadrifolié*
déci-	ten	*décimètre*	quinqu-	five	*quinquennal*
igni-	fire	*ignifugé*	quint-	fifth	*quintette*
lact-	milk	*lactique*	radio-	ray	*radiothérapie*
moto-	which moves	*motorisation*	uni-	one only	*uniforme*

■ Prefixes based on Greek words

Prefix	Meaning	Examples	Prefix	Meaning	Examples
aéro-	air	*aéronaute*	micro-	small	*microchirugie*
anthropo-	man	*anthropophage*	nécro-	death	*nécropole*
arché(o)-	antique	*archéologie*	néo-	new	*néologisme*
auto-	by itself	*automobile*	neuro-,	nerve	*neurochirurgie*
baro-	weighing	*baromètre*	nevr-		*névropathe*
biblio-	book	*bibliobus*	ophtalm-	eye	*ophtalmologie*
bio-	life	*biosphère*	oro-	mountain	*orogenèse*
caco-	bad	*cacophonie*	ortho-	right	*orthographe*
chrom(o)-	colour	*chromosome*	paléo-	old	*paléolithique*
chrono-	time	*chronologie*	pan-	all	*panthéisme*
chrys(o)-	gold	*chrysanthème*	pant(o)-		*pantomime*
cinémat(o)-	movement	*cinématographie*	patho-	sickness	*pathologie*
crypt(o)-	hidden	*cryptogramme*	ped-	infant	*pédagogie*
dactyl(o)-	finger	*dactylographie*	penta-	five	*pentagone*
déca-	ten	*décapode*	phago-	eat	*phagocyte*
dém(o)-	people	*démocrate*	phil(o)-	love	*philanthrope*
dynam(o)-	force	*dynamisme*	phon(o)-	voice	*phonogramme*
gaster-/tro-	stomach	*gastronome*	photo-	light	*photosynthèse*
gé(o)-	the earth	*géopolitique*	pneum(o)-	air, breath	*pneumatique*
hélio-	the sun	*héliogravure*	poly-	numerous	*polyglotte*
hémat(o)-,	blood	*hématurie*	pseud(o)-	false	*pseudonyme*
hémo-		*hémophile*	psych(o)-	mind	*psychothéraphie*
hipp(o)-	horse	*hippopotame*	pyr(o)-	fire	*pyrotechnie*
homéo-,	similar	*homéopathie*	techn(o)-	art	*technique*
hom(o)-		*homosexuel*	tétra-	four	*tétralogie*
hydr(o)-	water	*hydravion*	théo-	god	*théologie*
iso-	equal	*isotherme*	thermo-	heat	*thermomètre*
lith(o)	stone	*lithographie*	top(o)-	place	*toponymie*
macro-	big	*macrocéphale*	typo-	character	*typographe*
méga-	big	*mégawatt*	xén(o)-	foreigner	*xénophile*
més(o)	setting	*Mésopotamie*	xylo-	wood	*xylophone*
métr(o)-	measure	*métronome*	zoo-	animal	*zoologie*

THE MEANING OF WORDS

Each word has one or several meanings; the study of the meaning of words is known as semantics. Words which have several meanings are called "polysemantic"; thus, *pied*/foot has a proper meaning (*le pied de l'homme*/man's foot), and a figurative meaning (*un pied de table*/a table leg) and can also signify a unit of measure, etc. Words which have only one meaning are "monosemantic"; they are mainly scientific words.

EXPRESSIVE WORD FORMATION

Words which are called "expressive forms" are the diminutive, pejorative and onomatopoeic word forms.

• Diminutives, which are formed by adding a suffix, generally express the idea of smallness; they often add a nuance of affection or contempt:

men**otte**/handcuff, tiny hand, is a diminutive of *"main"*;

maisonn**ette**/small house, maisonnette, is a diminutive of *"maison"*;

femme**lette**/frail female/weakling (man), is a diminutive of *"femme"*.

• Pejorative or derogatory words, which are also formed by adding a suffix, express the contempt in which one holds the thing one is talking about. They are often considered familiar:

chauff**ard**/reckless driver, is a pejorative form of *"chauffeur"*/ driver;

popul**ace**/rabble, mob, is a pejorative form of *"peuple"*/people.

• Onomatopoeic words, which recall certain sounds, can become real nouns or be transformed into verbs:

(un) coucou/cuckoo; *(un) tic-tac*/ticking, to tick-tock; *patatras*/crash; *roucouler*/to coo; *ronronner*/to purr; *caqueter*/to prattle, to cackle.

LITERAL AND FIGURATIVE MEANING

Some words are sometimes used with an "image" meaning, which is different from their usual meaning:

*Un **chemin** est une voie de terre pour aller d'un lieu à un autre.*
A path is a track of land for going from one place to another.

"Chemin" is used here in its literal or "true" meaning.
In expressions like *le chemin du bonheur*/the road to happiness, *le chemin de la vie*/life's road, *"chemin"* is used in a figurative sense. Expressions like these, which enable us to create images, are called *"metaphors"*.

15

DEVELOPMENTS IN THE MEANING OF WORDS

Words do not always retain the same meaning during the history of a language. They can undergo changes; the main changes are the following.

● **Extension of meaning:** the word *"panier"* originally indicated a bread basket. Today it is a receptacle for carrying all sorts of things.

● **Restriction of meaning:** the verb *"émouvoir"* was used with the literal meaning of "to put into movement", "to move": *émouvoir des cloches*/to move (to ring) bells. Today it has only a figurative meaning: *un drame émouvant*/a moving drama or event.

● **Weakening of meaning:** the word *"triste"* used to mean shy, harmful. Today it means "sad", "sorrowful": *une triste nouvelle*/sad news, *des couleurs tristes*/sad colours.

● **Reinforcement of meaning:** the word *"génie"* used to mean "character". Today it means "the highest degree of intelligence or aptitude": *c'est un génie de la mécanique*/he's a genius at mechanics.

SYNONYMS AND ANTONYMS

Synonyms are words that mean almost the same thing, and can only be distinguished by fine shades of meaning:

*Une femme **fière** est soucieuse de son honneur et de sa dignité.*
A proud woman is concerned about her honour and dignity.

*Un homme **orgueilleux** admire ce qu'il fait et ce qu'il dit.*
An arrogant man admires what he does and what he says.

*Être **hautain**, c'est humilier les autres pour se grandir.*
To be haughty, means to humiliate others in order to feel superior.

*Être **altier**, c'est être impérieux et méprisant.*
To be superior, means to be imperious and contemptuous.

"Fier", *"orgueilleux"*, *"hautain"* et *"altier"* are synonyms.

Antonyms are words which have oppositive meanings:
grand et petit/big and small; *commencement et fin*/beginning and end; *monter et descendre*/go up and go down; *riche et pauvre*/rich and poor.

HOMONYMS

Homonyms are words which are pronounced in the same way although their spelling and their meaning are completely different, or which have the same spelling but different meanings: *sceau*/seal, *seau*/pail, *sot*/idiot and *saut*/jump are homonyms.
In the same way, the two words *"cousin"*, one meaning an insect (a mosquito) and the other meaning a relative (cousin), are homonyms.

NOTE : *Sceau, seau, sot, saut* are also called "homophones" because they are pronounced in the same way.
The two words *cousin* are also called "homographs" because they have the same spelling.

THE SENTENCE AND WORD CATEGORIES

The sentence is the basic unit of discourse; it is made of combinations of word groups, and has meaning. Words are distinguished according to their meaning, form and function in the sentence. Nouns, adjectives, articles, pronouns, verbs are variable words; adverbs, prepositions, conjunctions, interjections are invariable words. The noun and the verb are the essential constituants of the sentence. Respectively, they make up the noun group, which has a number of syntactic functions, and the verb group.

THE SENTENCE

▬THE SIMPLE SENTENCE

A simple sentence is made up solely of a noun group and a verb group:

Le chat *poursuit une souris.* / The cat is playing with a mouse.
   | |
noun group   verb group

Le petit chat de mon voisin *joue avec une pelote de laine.*
      | |
   noun group   verb group

My neighbour's cat is playing with a ball of wool.

It can be seen that each group can be developed using adjectives or other groups of words with a complementary function and creating a branching of the simple sentence.

Conversely, it can happen that a noun group is reduced to a single noun;

Marie *joue avec Jean.*/Marie is playing with John.
  |
noun group

Sometimes, the verb group is reduced to a single verb:

Le petit chat *dort.*/The little cat is sleeping.
        |
        verb group

Sometimes, the noun group is not expressed, when, for example, the verb is in the imperative:

Viens ici!/Come here!

However, sometimes the noun group signifying the person being addressed can be expressed:

Paul, viens ici!/Paul, come here!

▬THE COMPLEX SENTENCE

A complex sentence is made up of a combination of a number of clauses, known as "*propositions*" in French; these clauses are subordinated to the simple sentence, which is known as the main sentence, by means of conjunctions and relative pronouns:

Je pense	que	Paul a dû être retardé par l'orage.
Main clause	conjunction	subordinate clause

I think Paul has been delayed by the storm.
(See chapter on clauses and following chapters.)

GRAMMATICAL CATEGORIES

Combining words in a sentence in order to create meaning is carried out according to rules specific to the different grammatical categories to which the words belong.
Each word belongs to a grammatical category, defined by its syntactic and semantic properties.

● **The verb** expresses an action or a state:

Le jardin reste inculte depuis qu'elle est partie. ("rester" = state verb)
The garden has remained uncared for, since she left.

Il part en vacances demain. ("partir" = action verb)
He goes on holiday tomorrow.

● **The noun** signifies a person or a thing which is in a state, which takes part in an action, which is in relation with another person or thing:

Depuis plusieurs jours, les vagues frappaient la digue avec violence.
For several days now, the waves have been crashing violently on the sea wall.

● **The article** determines the noun and identifies its gender and number:

Un concert sera donné dans la salle des fêtes.
A concert will be given in the village hall.

● **The adjective** indicates a quality or determines the noun:

Un fin voilier entre dans le port.
An elegant sailing boat enters the port.

Ma sœur a lu ce livre deux fois.
My sister has read this book twice.

● **The pronoun** replaces the noun or indicates the person who acts or undergoes the action:

J'ai prêté mon stylo à Luce, car elle avait perdu le sien.
I lent my pen to Luce, because she had lost her own.

● **The adverb** changes the meaning of an adjective, a verb or another adverb:

Elle s'installe confortablement.
She is settling in comfortably.

Il fait trop beau pour travailler.
The weather is too good for working.

"Très peu, dit-il".
"Very little, he said".

● **The conjunction** and **the preposition** establish the relationship between words or groups of words:

> Les parents **et** les amis **de** Jean le félicitèrent **pour** sa promotion.
> John's parents and friends congratulated him on his promotion.

● **The interjection** highlights an exclamation of anger, surprise, contempt, etc.:

> **Hélas!** tout est perdu!
> Alas! All is lost!

> **Oh!** il n'est pas rentré!
> Oh! he has not come back!

CHANGES IN GRAMMATICAL CATEGORY

A word is originally either a noun, an adjective or a verb, but it can change its grammatical category:
– a noun can become an adjective:

> griller des **marrons** → des vestes **marron** (colour adjective)
> to roast chesnuts → brown jackets

– an adjective can become a noun, an adverb, or a preposition:

> elle est **malade** → soigner les **malades** (noun)
> she is sick → to nurse the patients

> un **faux** pas → il chante **faux** (adverb)
> a mistake → he sings out of tune

> il est sain et **sauf** → **sauf** votre respect
> he is safe and sound → save your respect

– the participle can become an adjective, a noun, or a preposition:

> **obéissant** à sa mère → une fille **obéissante** (adjective)
> obeying her mother → an obedient daughter

> **assuré** contre le vol → les **assurés** sociaux (noun)
> insured against theft → people with social security

> en **suivant** la route → **suivant** ce qu'il dira (preposition)
> by following the road → according to what he says

– an infinitive can become a noun:

> elle croit **devoir** le dire → elle fait son **devoir**
> she believes she must say it → she does her duty

– an adverb can become a noun, or an adjective:

> rester **dehors** → des **dehors** insignifiants (noun)
> stay outside → unsignificant appearances

> il dort **bien** → des gens très **bien** (adjective)
> he sleeps well → very nice people

PUNCTUATION

Punctuation marks help to separate sentences, clauses, words between each other, in order to create greater clarity, to show shades of meaning, or to add emphasis.

● **The full stop or period (.)** indicates the end of the sentence:

La maison est au sommet de la colline.
The house is on top of the hill.

● **The comma (,)** separates parts of discourse which are in juxtaposition or apposition: subjects, verbs, adjectives, etc., or adverbial clauses, defining relative clauses, interpolated and participial clauses. It indicates a short pause:

On voit le ciel, la mer, la côte.
You can see the sky, the sea, the coast.

Cette maison, vieille, massive, sorte de forteresse, était inhabitée.
This old, massive house, a kind of fortrees, was uninhabited.

Je vois, dit-il, que vous comprenez.
I see, he said, that you understand.

● **The semi-colon (;)** separates two aspects of the same idea, two stages of an action. It indicates a slightly longer pause than the comma:

Le chien, qui sommellait, s'éveilla en sursaut ; il dressa l'oreille.
The dog, who was dozing, suddenly woke up; he cocked his ear.

● **The question mark (?)** is placed at the end of a sentence expressing a direct question:

Quand aurons-nous terminé ?   *Que veut-elle ?*
When will we have finished?   What does she want?

● **The exclamation mark (!)** is placed after interjections or a sentence expressing strong feelings:

Attention !   *Comme je vous plains !*
Watch out!   How I pity you!

● **The dash (—)** indicates the beginning of a dialogue or a change in speaker; it is also used to highlight a word or group of words:

— *Es-tu prête ? — Pas encore.*
— Are you ready? — Not yet.

L'autre chien — le vieux — dormait.
The other dog — the old one — was sleeping.

● **Suspension marks (...)** indicate that the thinking has not been completely expressed. They also indicate a pause highlighting what follows:

Si elle avait voulu...
If she had wanted...

Cette absence me paraît... surprenante.
This absence seems to me... surprising.

● **Inverted commas or quotes (« »)** are placed at the beginning and at the end of a quotation or the direct reporting of someone's words, or to indicate that an expression is foreign in everyday language:

« Venez me voir demain », dit-il.
"Come and see me tomorrow", he said.

La « polenta » est un mets italien.
"Polenta" is an Italian dish.

● **The colon (:)** precedes a quotation or an explanatory development:

Elle s'écria : "Lâchez-moi!"
She cried out: "Let go of me!"

Je n'avance pas : je suis sans cesse dérangé.
I am not getting on: I keep being interrupted.

● **Parenthesis or brackets ()** indicate an accessory sentence or afterthought, or encloses the name of an author after a quotation:

On annonça (et chacun s'en doutait) que le vainqueur ne viendrait pas.
It was anounced (and everyone had suspected it) that the winner would not be coming.

Rien ne sert de courir, il faut partir à point. (La Fontaine)
It's no use running, you just have to start on time.

● **Square brackets [ ]** are sometimes used in place of parenthesis, for example, to add precision, or a personal remark within a quotation:

Elle [la cigale] alla crier famine... (La Fontaine)
She [the cicada] cried out she was starving...

PART II
PARTS OF SPEECH

THE NOUN

The noun, also called the substantive, is a variable word, which indicates either something animate (person or animal) or something inanimate (object or idea): *chat*/cat, *table*/table, *informaticienne*/computer specialist, *honneur*/honour, *sentiment*/ feeling are nouns.

DIFFERENT CATEGORIES OF NOUNS

We can distinguish, according to meaning:
– concrete nouns, which indicate living things or objects;
– abstract nouns, which indicate ideas, manners of being:

> *navire*/boat is a concrete noun; *fermeté*/firmness is an abstract noun.

We can distinguish, according to form:
– single nouns, formed from a single word:

> *timbre*/stamp is a single noun;

– compound nouns, formed by joining several words (see above):

> *portemanteau*/coathanger is a compound noun written as one word;

> *timbre-poste*/postage stamp is a compound noun written in separate words, with a hyphen.

> *résidence secondaire*/second house is a compound noun written in separate words, with no hypen.

COMMON NOUNS AND PROPER NOUNS

Nouns can be divided into common nouns and proper nouns.
Common nouns indicate beings, things of the same kind:

> *fauteuil*/armchair is a common noun; it indicates a particular object, but also a general class of objects; "*fauteuil*" is common to all objects of the same kind. It does not take a capital letter.

Proper nouns give living things, or personified objects a personality which presents them as individuals distinct from others:

> *Louise, un Québécois, le Saint-Laurent, Lausanne, le Sénégal* are proper nouns. They take a capital letter.

Proper nouns are for the most part first names, family names, names of inhabitants of a country, of a region or town and geographical names (countries, rivers, mountains, regions, etc.).

⚠ A proper noun is sometimes used as a common noun and vice-versa:

Le **bordeaux** est un vin de la région de **Bordeaux**.
A bordeaux wine is a wine that comes from the Bordeaux region.

Hercule est un héros mythologique. Un **hercule** est un homme très fort.
Hercules is a a mythological hero.   A hercules is a very strong man.

On the other hand the family names *Charpentier, Lemercier, Marchand* are proper nouns originating from common nouns.

GENDER

Nouns divide into two genders, masculine and feminine, which are shown by the agreement of the articles and adjectives which go with them:

le frère/brother (masculine); *la* sœur/sister (feminine);

un pantalon blanc/white trousers; *une* robe blanche/a white dress.

The nouns of human beings and of certain animals are masculine or feminine according to their sex:

le père/father; *la* mère/mother; *le* soldat/soldier;

la concierge/concierge; *le* chien/dog; *la* chienne/bitch.

⚠ *Une ordonnance*/a medical prescription, *une vigie*/a lookout, a vigil, *une estafette*/a courier, *une sentinelle*/a sentry, when referring to men, are put in the feminine, whereas *un mannequin*/mannequin, *un bas-bleu*/a blue stocking, *un laideron*/an ugly duckling and *un cordon-bleu*, when referring to women, are put in the masculine.

Object nouns and abstract nouns are placed according to usage in one or the other of the genders:

une table/a table, *un* banc/a bench, *une* chaise/a chair, *un* lit/a bed.

Certain suffixes or endings help to identify the gender of nouns:

Masculine noun suffixes	Examples	Feminine noun suffixes	Examples
-age	le nettoyage	-ade	une baignade
-ail	le travail	-aie	une cerisaie
-ain	un Romain	-aille	une canaille
-ament	le firmament	-aine	une quinzaine
-eau	un bordereau	-aison	une salaison
-ement	l'étonnement	-ance	la croyance
-er	un boucher	-ande	une réprimande
-ier	un prunier	-ée	une visée

Masculine noun suffixes	Examples	Feminine noun suffixes	Examples
-illon	un raidillon	-ie	de la charcuterie
-in	un ravin	-ille	une brindille
-is	du hachis	-ise	la franchise
-isme	le racisme	-ison	une garnison
-oir	le terroir	-itude	la solitude
-teur	un alternateur	-oire	une écumoire
		-sion	la passion
		-té	la beauté
		-tion	une attention
		-trice	une motrice
		-ure	la culture

Certain categories of nouns belong to a particular gender.
The following are usually masculine:
– the names of trees: **un** *chêne*/an oak tree, **un** *pin*/a pine tree, **un** *hêtre*/a beech tree;
– the names of metals: **le** *fer*/iron, **le** *zinc*/zinc, **le** *cuivre*/copper;
– the names of languages: **le** *français*/French, **le** *chinois*/Chinese, **le** *turc*/Turkish.
The following are usually feminine:
– the names of sciences: **la** *physique*/physics, **la** *chimie*/chemistry, with the exception: **le** *droit*/law.

NUMBER

Nouns can be either singular or plural; the singular indicates one being only or one object; the plural indicates several beings or objects:

un *chat*/cat (singular); **des** *chats*/cats (plural).

However, some nouns, called "collective nouns", indicate in the singular a group of beings or things:

le *bétail*/cattle; **la** *foule*/the crowd; **la** *flotte marchande*/the merchant navy.

Some nouns are used only in the plural; some of them indicate an ensemble:

des *archives*/archives; **des** *bestiaux*/livestock; **des** *décombres*/rubble, debris;

but others do not specifically convey the idea of plurality:

les *ténèbres*/darkness; **les** *arrhes*/a deposit.

THE FEMININE FORM OF NOUNS

If certain things are feminine by nature, others indicating human beings or animals, show two forms: masculine and feminine.

We say that a noun has variable gender when it has both a masculine and a feminine form.

FORMING THE FEMININE

In general, the feminine of a noun is formed by simple adding an -e to the end of the masculine form:

un ami/a friend → *une amie*; *un cousin*/a cousin → *une cousine*.

Nouns ending in **-e** in the masculine do not change in the feminine: *un artiste*/an artist→ *une artiste*, except a few which make their feminine form with the suffix **-esse**: *un prince*/a prince → *une princesse*.

⚠ ● Some nouns ending in **-t** in the masculine double the **-t** in the feminine: *un chat*/a cat → *une chatte*. Similarly, *"paysan"*/a peasant and *"Jean"* double the -n in the feminine: *une paysanne, Jeanne*.

● Other nouns make their feminine form in a special way, either by using a special suffix, or by doubling or changing the final consonant of the masculine form or by introducing an accent:

Masculine ending	Feminine ending	Examples
-eau	-elle	*un jumeau, une jumelle*
-el	-elle	*Gabriel, Gabrielle*
-er	-ère	*un fermier, une fermière*
		un boucher, une bouchère
-eur	-euse	*un danseur, une danseuse*
	-eresse	*un vengeur, une vengeresse*
-f	-ve	*un veuf, une veuve*
-ien	-ienne	*un gardien, une gardienne*
-ion	-ionne	*un lion, une lionne*
-oux	-ouse	*un époux, une épouse*
-p	-ve	*un loup, une louve*

IRREGULAR FEMININE

Sometimes the word indicating the feminine form of a noun can be very or totally different from the masculine form.
For example:

roi,	reine	serviteur,	servante	empereur,	impératrice
mari,	femme	parrain,	marraine	fils,	fille
gendre,	bru	dieu,	déesse	neveu,	nièce
duc,	duchesse	héros,	héroïne	frère,	sœur
oncle,	tante	bélier,	brebis	verrat,	truie
jars,	oie	lièvre,	hase	cerf,	biche

25

Certain nouns, mainly referring to the professions, do not as yet have a corresponding feminine form; in these cases the word *"femme"*/woman is added to the noun: *un médecin*/doctor → *une femme médecin.*
But sometimes there is a separate feminine form: *un avocat*/lawyer → *une avocate.*

NOTE : Some nouns, designating animals, only exist in the masculine or in the feminine; if we wish to indicate the sex of the animals precisely, we have to add the words *"mâle"* or *"femelle"*: *un serpent femelle*/female snake; *une hirondelle mâle*/male swallow.

SPECIAL CASES OF NOUN GENDER

● Some nouns change gender when they move from the singular to the plural:

– *amour* is masculine in the singular and often feminine in the plural:

　　*un grand amour; de **folles** amours*/a great love; crazy love**s**

– *délice* is masculine in the singular and feminine in the plural:

　　Ce gâteau est un pur délice. C'étaient sans cesse des nouvelles délices. This cake is a sheer delight. There were continuous new delights.

– *orgue* is masculine in the singular and feminine in the plural (indicating one musical instrument):

　　un orgue excellent; jouer aux grandes orgues
　　an excellent organ; to play the great organs

● Some nouns hesitate between the two genders, for example, *après-midi*/afternoon, *entre-deux-guerres*/interwar period, *palabre*/palaver, *pamplemousse*/grapefruit, *parka*/parka: *un bel* après-midi or *une belle* après-midi.

● *Gens*/people is normally masculine: *Il y a des gens très courageux.*/ There are some very courageous people.

⚠ In some expressions: *les bonnes gens*/good people, *les petites gens*/little people, the word *"gens"* is preceded by an adjective in the feminine, but followed by an attributive adjective in the masculine: *les vieilles gens sont polis*/old people are polite.

● *Chose* and *personne* are feminine nouns, but when used as indefinite pronouns, they are in the masculine, for example:

　　*une chose claire; **quelque chose** de clair*
　　a clear thing; something clear

● Some nouns have a different meaning when in the masculine or in the feminine, for example: *un **manœuvre*** is an unskilled worker; *une **manœuvre*** is a military exercise or movement.

THE PLURAL OF NOUNS

As a general rule, a noun can take two forms: singular and plural. We say the noun is variable with regard to number. The singular indicates a single being or single thing, and the plural several beings or several things.

PLURAL OF COMMON NOUNS

In most cases, the plural of common nouns is made by adding an **-s** to the singular:

un ennui/a problem → *des ennuis*; *un lit*/a bed → *des lits*.

⚠ The plural and the singular are the same for nouns ending in **-s**, **-x**, **-z**:

un bois → *des bois*; *une noix* → *des noix*; *un nez* → *des nez*
a wood → woods; a walnut → walnuts; a nose → noses.

● Nouns ending in **-al** have **-aux** in the plural. However, *bal*/ball, *carnaval*/carnival, *cérémonial*/ceremonial, *chacal*/jackal, *choral*/chorale, *festival*/festival, *pal*/stake, *récital*/recital, *régal*/treat, *santal*/sandalwood, etc. follow the general rule:

un cheval/a horse → des chev**aux**; *un chacal* → des chacal**s**.

● The plural of nouns ending in **-eau, -au, -eu** and **-œu** are formed by adding an **-x** to the singular. Exceptions are: *landau*/baby carriage, *sarrau*/smock, *bleu*/bruise, *pneu*/tyre, which take an **-s** in the plural:

un veau/a calf → *des veaux*; *un feu*/a fire → *des feux*;
un vœu/a wish → *des vœux*; *un étau*/a vice → *des étaux*;
un pneu/a tyre → *des pneus*.

● In general, the plural of nouns ending in **-ou** is **-ous**. Exceptions are: *bijou*/jewel, *caillou*/pebble, *chou*/cabbage, *genou*/knee, *hibou*/owl, *pou*/louse, which take an **-x** in the plural:

un cou/a neck → *des cous*; *un chou* → *des choux*.

● Nouns whose singular ends in **-ail** have a regular plural in **-ails**. Except *bail*/lease, *corail*/coral, *émail*/enamel, *soupirail*/basement window, *travail*/work, *vantail*/swing door, *vitrail*/stained glass window, which have **-aux** in the plural:

un rail/a rail → *des rails*; *un travail* → *des travaux*.

● The nouns *aïeul*/grand parent, *ciel*/sky and *œil*/eye have irregular plurals:

l'aïeul → *les aïeux*; *le ciel* → *les cieux*; *l'œil* → *les yeux*.

⚠ We say *bisaïeuls*, *trisaïeuls* and *aïeuls* with the meaning of "great grandparents", *ciels* in "*ciels de lit*", "*les ciels d'Île-de-France*", and *œils* in "*œils de bœuf*".

PLURAL OF COMMON NOUNS OF FOREIGN ORIGIN

The plural of nouns borrowed from other languages is formed according to the general rule for common nouns:

un référendum → *des référendums.*

Some of these nouns have kept the plural from the foreign language as well as the French plural; but the latter tends to be more usual now:

un maximum → *des maxima* or *des maximums*;
un gentleman → *des gentlemen* or *des gentlemans*;
un lied → *des lieder* or *des lieds*.

PLURAL OF PROPER NOUNS

GEOGRAPHICAL NOUNS

The plural of geographical nouns is formed like that of common nouns:

la Guyane française → *les Guyanes*; *l'Amérique* → *les Amériques.*

NAMES OF PEOPLE

People's names take the plural ending:

● when they signify:
– royal families: *les Bourbons, les Tudors*;
– famous families: *les Condés, les Ségurs*;

● when they serve as models or as a type: *les Hugos*, les *Pasteurs.*

⚠ Proper names remain unchanged when they are used in a grandiloquent way with the definite article:

Les **Molière** et les **Racine** sont l'image de leur temps.
Molière and Racine are the image of their time.

PLURAL OF COMPOUND NOUNS

COMPOUND NOUNS WRITTEN AS ONE WORD

They form their plural like that of single nouns:

un entresol → *des entresols*; *un gendarme* → *des gendarmes.*

⚠ We say *gentilshommes, bonshommes, messieurs, mesdames, mesdemoiselles, messeigneurs,* for the plural of *gentilhomme, bonhomme, monsieur, madame, mademoiselle, monseigneur.*

■COMPOUND NOUNS WRITTEN AS SEPARATE WORDS

● If the compound nouns are formed with an adjective and a noun, both elements show the plural ending:

> *un coffre-fort*/security safe → *des coffres-forts;*
> *une basse-cour*/farmyard → *des basses-cours;*
> *un château fort*/fortified castle → *des châteaux forts.*

● If they are formed by two nouns in apposition, both elements show the plural ending:

> *un chou-fleur*/cauliflower → *des choux-fleurs;*
> *un chef-lieu*/county town → *des chefs-lieux.*

● If they are formed by a noun followed by a noun complement, either introduced by a preposition or not, the first noun only shows the plural ending:

> *un chef-d'œuvre*/masterpiece, *des chefs-d'œuvre;*
> *un timbre-poste*/postage stamp, *des timbres-poste;*
> *une pomme de terre*/potato, *des pommes de terre.*

● If they are formed by an invariable word and a noun, the noun only takes the plural ending:

> *une avant-garde*/vanguard → *des avant-gardes;*
> *un en-tête*/letter heading → *des en-têtes.*

● If they are formed from two verbs or from an expression, all the words remain unchanged:

> *un va-et-vient*/coming and going → *des va-et-vient;*
> *un tête-à-tête*/private conversation → *des tête-à-tête.*

● If they are made up of a verb and its complement, the verb remains unchanged and the noun usually remains in the singular (as in the compounds formed with **abat-, porte-, presse-**):

> *un abat-jour*/lampshade → *des abat-jour;*
> *un presse-papier*/paperweight → *des presse-papier;*
> *un porte-plume*/pen rest → *des porte-plume;*
> *un cache-col*/muffler → *des cache-col;*
> *un gratte-ciel*/skyscraper → *des gratte-ciel.*

⚠ For a certain number of nouns made up in this way, the nouns take the plural:

> *un couvre-lit*/a bedspread → *des couvre-lits* (bedcover);
> *un tire-bouchon*/corkscrew → *des tire-bouchons.*

● In the compound nouns with the word ***garde***, this latter can either be a noun or a verb. If it is a noun, it takes the plural ending and the following noun remains unchanged; if it is a verb it remains unchanged and the noun following may or may not take the plural ending according to the meaning:

*un garde-chasse/*gamekeeper → *des gardes-chasse(s) ("garde"* refers to the person responsible for looking after the wild game);

*un garde-boue/*mudguard → *des garde-boue* (here *"garde"* is a verb: the compound noun designates an object which guards or protects against mud).

● In compound nouns with the adjective **grand**, this latter used to remain unchanged if it was accompanied by a feminine noun:

*une grand-mère/*grandmother → *des grand-mères*;
but *un grand-père/*grandfather → *des grands-pères*.

However, today we write: *une grand-mère → des grands-mères*.

Change of meaning in the plural

Over time some nouns have acquired different meanings in the singular and the plural:

Le sculpteur se sert d'un ciseau.
A sculpter uses a chisel.

On utilise les ciseaux pour couper le papier.
One uses scissors to cut paper.

Similarly:

*assise/*basis	*assises/*meeting
*lunette/*telescope	*lunettes/*spectacles
*vacance/*vacancy	*vacances/*holidays

THE NOUN SUBJECT AND AGENT

In order to find the subject of a verb, we ask the question "who is it?" or "what is it?" and put it before the verb of the sentence. For example, in *Paule tombe.*/ Paule falls down., we can ask: "who is it that falls down?" *Paule*. *"Paule"* is the subject of *"tombe"*.

In *La boue tache les jambes.*/The mud dirties the legs., what is it that dirties? *La boue*. *"Boue"* is the subject of *"tache"*. When a verb moves from the active voice to the passive voice, the subject of the verb becomes the agent of the passive verb.

MEANING AND FUNCTION OF A SUBJECT NOUN

● A noun is the subject of a verb when it designates the person or the thing which carries out the action or which is in the state indicated by the active verb:

Les arbres **perden**t *leurs feuilles en automne./* The trees lose their
⎮   leaves in the autumn.
subject of *"perdent"*

Le **vent** *se lève./* The wind is rising.: *"vent"* is the subject of *"se lève"*.

● A noun is the subject of a passive verb when it indicates the person or the thing which undergoes the action indicated by the verb:

Le discours **fut prononcé** *par le maire./* The speech was given by
⎮   the mayor.
subject of *"fut prononcé"*

THE SUBJECT OF A VERB
IN A PERSONAL OR NON-PERSONAL MOOD

● A noun can be the subject of a verb in a personal mood: indicative, conditional and subjunctive:

Les **assistants se mirent** à rire./The assistants started to laugh.:
"assistant" is the subject of *"se mirent"*.

● It can also be the subject of the infinitive, the verb in the infinitive proposition:

Elle vit l'**avion atterrir** sur la piste./She saw the plane land on the runway.: *"l'avion"* is the subject of *"atterrir"*;

or subject of the infinitive of narration:

Grenouilles aussitôt **de sauter** dans les ondes. (La Fontaine)/The frogs immediately jumped into the water.: *"grenouilles"* is the subject of *"sauter"*.

● A noun can also be the subject of a participle, the verb of the participial clause:

> Le **repas fini**, *elle prit son journal.*/The meal over, she picked up the newspaper.: *"repas"* is the subject of *"(étant) fini"*.

NON-EXPRESSED SUBJECT

The subject is not expressed when the verb is in the imperative, or in expressions which go back to old French:

> **Allons** *voir ce qui se passe.*/Let's see what is happening.
> *Peu* **importe**. (means: *Il importe peu.*/it matters little.)

REAL SUBJECT AND APPARENT SUBJECT

With impersonal verbs or verbs used impersonally (see "Moods and tenses"), we distinguish between the apparent subject and the real subject. The real subject, placed after the verb, carries out or undergoes the action indicated by the verb.

The apparent subject is a pronoun (*il* or *ce*) which, placed before the verb, indicates the real subject, and dictates the agreement of the verb:

> *Il lui arrive une aventure extraordinaire.*/A strange adventure has happened to him.
>
> apparent subject   real subject of *"arrive"*
> of *"arrive"*

> **C'**est une maligne, cette fille./She's smart, that girl.: *"c'"* is the apparent subject of *"est"*; *"fille"* is the real subject of *"est"*.

THE NOUN AS AGENT

The agent of the verb answers the question "by whom", placed after a verb in the passive.
It expresses the agent by whom the action is carried out:

> *Elle fut heurtée* **par un passant**./She was knocked into by a passerby.

If the same idea were expressed in the active voice, the agent of the passive voice would become the subject of the active verb: **Un passant** *la heurta.*/A passerby knocked into her.

The agent can be introduced by the prepositions:

– **de**: *Il est aimé de ses parents.*/He is loved by his parents. *Il est compris de tous.*/He is understood by everybody.;

– **par**: *Sa maison fut pillée par des voleurs.*/His house was pillaged by thieves.

POSITION OF THE SUBJECT NOUN

The subject is normally placed before the verb:

Le **jardinier** `gardait` *ses fleurs.*/The gardener looked after his flowers.
Le **chat** `dort` *près du feu.*/The cat is sleeping near the fire.

⚠ The subject can change position; this is referred to as "subject inversion".

POSITION AFTER THE VERB

● The noun subject is placed after the verb:

– in direct questions which begin with the interrogative pronoun **que**, attribute or direct object, or by the interrogative adjective **quel**:

Que `veut` **ce client**?/What does this customer want?
Quel est votre avis?/ What is your opinion?

– in inserted clauses:

Je ne pourrai, `répondit` **Pierre**, *venir demain à notre rendez-vous.*
I shall not, Pierre replied, be able to come to our meeting tomorrow.

– in propositions indicating a wish or a hypothesis, or starting with the expressions **peu importe, qu'importe?**:

`Puisse` **votre pronostic** *se réaliser!*/May your forecast come true!

`Soit` **le cercle** *de centre O.*/Let us assume a circle with a centre O.
Peu importe **mon plaisir!**/My pleasure matters little!

– in propositions beginning with an attributive adjective:

Tel `est` **mon conseil**./That is my advice.

Rares `sont` **les exceptions**./There are rare exceptions.

● The subject noun can be placed after the verb, without this being an obligatory structure:

– in relative clauses beginning with a direct object relative, an attribute or an adverbial phrase:

la chanson que `chantait` **Paule**, *or la chanson que* **Paule** `chantait`
the song that Paule was singing

– in infinitive propositions (see "the completives"):

J'ai entendu `chanter` **le coq**. *or J'ai entendu* **le coq** `chanter`.
I heard the cock crow.

– in indirect interrogative clauses starting with a question word (**quel**, **quand**, **comment**, etc.):

Je ne me rappelle plus où `habitait` **Jacques**, *or où* **Jacques** `habitait`.
I can't remember where Jacques lived.

– in clauses beginning with an adverb or an adverbial clause of time or place:

> *Le long d'un clair ruisseau* buvait *une colombe*. (La Fontaine)
> By the side of a clear stream a dove was drinking.

– in some subordinate conjunctives:

> *comme* croient *les enfants or comme les enfants* croient
> as children believe.

▬▬POSITION OF THE SUBJECT NOUN BEFORE THE VERB AND REITERATED BY A PRONOUN

● The subject noun is placed before the verb, but is taken up again by a personal pronoun after the verb (or between the auxiliary and the verb):

– in direct interrogative clauses which do not begin with a question word, or are introduced by the interrogative pronoun *qui*, direct object, or by the adverb *pourquoi*:

> *Qui le conseil a-t-il élu président?*
> Who did the council elect chairman?

> *Pourquoi votre sœur ne m'a-t-elle rien dit?*
> Why did your sister say nothing to me?

– in direct interrogative clauses where the question does not refer to the direct object:

> *Comment votre mère a-t-elle appris la nouvelle?*
> How did your mother learn the news?

In a sentence like this, the question does not refer to *"la nouvelle"*, which is the direct object, but rather to the manner in which it is learned.

● The subject noun can be put in front of the verb, but taken up again by a personal pronoun placed after the verb (or between the auxiliary and the verb), without this structure being obligatory:

– in propositions beginning with the adverbs *du moins, au moins, ainsi, peut-être, aussi, à peine, sans doute*:

> *Du moins Paule n'a-t-elle rien vu.* or *Du moins Paule n'a rien vu.*
> At least Paule saw nothing.

– in interrogative clauses which begin with the adverbs *où, quand, comment, combien* or by the the interrogative pronouns *qui* or *quoi* when these are indirect objects or adverbial phrases:

> *Où cette route mène-t-elle?* or *Où mène cette route?*
> Where does this road lead to?

– in exclamative clauses starting with an exclamation (but, in this case, without reiteration by a pronoun):

> *Que d'efforts ce travail a exigés!* or *Que d'efforts a exigés ce travail!/* What a lot of effort this work took!

THE DETERMINING COMPLEMENT

A determining complement is a word or group of words which makes clear the meaning of another word, limits its extent and determines it. If the word which has been determined is a noun, then we speak about a noun complement. There are also determining complements for adjectives and adverbs (see pages 59 and 139).

PLACE OF THE NOUN COMPLEMENT

The noun complement is part of the noun group. It is always placed after the noun it determines, and is usually linked by a preposition.

Le lion est le roi de la savane./The lion is the king of the savannah.

preposition   article   noun complement of *"roi"*

But it can also be placed simply alongside:

*une moquette **polyester*** (= *en polyester*)/a polyester carpet.

MEANING OF NOUN COMPLEMENT

The noun complement can express:

– the owner or the author: *une lettre de **Pierre**/a letter from Peter*
– the subject of the action: *l'arrivée des **coureurs**/the arrival of the runners*
– the object of the action: *l'invention d'un **procédé**/the invention of a process*

– physical material: *une montre en **or**/a gold watch*
– the purpose, the destination: *une trousse à **outils**/a tool kit*
– the location: *la bataille d'**Angleterre**/the Battle of Britain*
– the origin: *le jambon d'**York**/York ham*

– the contents: *la bouteille de **lait**/the bottle of milk*
– the whole ensemble of which the completed noun forms only a part: *les doigts de la **main**; les voiles du **navire*** the fingers of the hand; the sails of the ship
– the quality: *le héron au long **bec**/the long-beaked heron*
– the means, the manner: *un coup de **couteau**/a knife blow*
– the measure, the price: *un fossé de trois **mètres**; un livre de grand **prix*** a trench three metres wide; a high priced book

The noun complement is most often introduced by the preposition ***de***, but it can also be introduced by ***à, en, par, pour***, etc., according to meaning:

*le ronronnement **du** chat; la lutte **pour** la vie*
the purring of the cat; the struggle for life

THE NOUN AS OBJECT

A noun has the role of object when it indicates the being or the thing which is the object of the action expressed by the verb. In the sentence *Le vent gonfle les voiles.*/The wind fills the sails., *"voiles"* is the object of *"gonfle"*. In *Tu dois te souvenir de nos jeunes années.*/You must recall our early years., *"années"* is the object of *"te souvenir"*.

THE DIFFERENT KINDS OF OBJECT

There are three types of objects.

• The direct object which is constructed without a preposition:

J'ai fermé la fenêtre *.*/I closed the window.

direct object of *"j'ai fermé"*

• The indirect object, which is introduced by a preposition, usually *à* or *de*:

Ils renoncèrent à la poursuite./They gave up the pursuit.
indirect object of *"renoncèrent"*

Je n'ai jamais douté de ses capacités./I never doubted his abilities.: *"capacités"* is the indirect object of *"ai douté"*.

NOTE : Only through usage can we tell which verb takes which preposition; *obéir à, jouer de, échapper à, user de, nuire à*, etc.

• The second object which we can find with certain verbs that already have a direct or indirect object:

On a opposé un refus à ma demande *.*/My request met with a refusal.

second object of *"a opposé"*

J'ai parlé de cette question à un spécialiste./I spoke to a specialist about this question.: *"spécialiste"* is the second object of *"j'ai parlé"*.

NOTE : We use the name attributive complement for a second object of a verb which expresses the idea of giving, lending, giving back, selling, belonging, granting, awarding:

Il a loué sa maison à des étrangers./He rented his house to some foreigners.: *"étrangers"* is the attributive complement of *"a loué"*.

POSITION OF THE NOUN OBJECT

The noun object is normally positioned after the verb:

Elle avait terminé la lecture de ce livre.
She had finished reading this book.

In interrogative or exclamative sentences, the noun object can be placed before the verb if the question or exclamation refers to the object:

> *Quelle **route** dois-je suivre?*/Which road must I follow?: *"route"* is the direct object of *"suivre"*.

> *De quelle **route** parlez-vous?*/Which road are you talking about?: *"route"* is the indirect object of *"parlez"*.

> *Quel **bruit** vous faites!*/What a noise you are making!: *"bruit"* is the direct object of *"faites"*.

The noun object can be placed at the beginning of the sentence to give it greater emphasis, but in this case it must be taken up again by a personal pronoun:

> *Cette **décision**, je **la** réprouve.*/This decision I disapprove.: *"décision"* is the direct object of *"réprouve"*, like *"la"* which reiterates *"décision"*.

THE NOUN PREDICATE, APPOSITION AND APOSTROPHE

A noun, whether acting as a subject or an object, can be qualified and specifically determined in ways other than by using an adjective (see page 58) or a determining complement.

THE PREDICATIVE NOUN

A noun is predicative when it indicates the quality given or recognized in a subject or an object, through the intermediary of the verb.

THE PREDICATIVE SUBJECT

The predicate of the subject is introduced by a verb of state (*être*, *paraître*, *sembler*, etc.), by certain verbs in the passive or by certain intransitive verbs:

Tout vous est aquilon, tout me semble zéphyr. (La Fontaine): "*aquilon*" and "*zéphyr*" are predicates of each "*tout*" subject.

Elle a été élue déléguée./She has been elected delegate.: "*déléguée*" is the predicate of the subject "*elle*".

Paul restait un enfant./Paul remained a child.: "*enfant*" is a predicate of the subject "*Paul*".

THE PREDICATIVE OBJECT

The predicate of an object is introduced by a verb like *croire*, *estimer*, *faire*, *juger*, *penser*, *nommer*, *rendre*, *voir*, *choisir*, *élire*, *trouver*, etc.:

Je le crois honnête homme./I believe him to be an honest man.: "*honnête homme*" is the predicate of the object "*le*".

Le roi l'a fait duc et pair./The king made him a duke and a peer.: "*duc*" and "*pair*" are predicates of the object "*l'*".

⚠ The predicate of a subject or an object can be introduced by a preposition (*pour*, *en*, *de*) or by a conjunction (*comme*):

On l'a pris pour un fou./He was taken for a madman.: "*fou*" is the predicate of the object "*l'*".

Elle me traite en ami./She treats me like a friend.: "*ami*" is the predicate of the object "*me*".

Il est considéré comme un savant./He is considered a learned man.: "*savant*" is a predicate of the subject "*il*".

THE NOUN IN APPOSITION

A noun is placed in apposition when it is joined (usually without using a preposition) to another noun — or a pronoun — in order to indicate its quality, to define it and make it more precise. The apposition refers to the same person or the same thing as the noun it completes.

Very often the noun in apposition is separated from the word it completes by a pause (a comma in the written form):

le lion, **terreur** *de la savane*/the lion, terror of the savannah: "*terreur*" is placed in apposition to "*lion*".

Vous, les **élèves** *de cette classe…*/You, the pupils of this class…: "*élèves*" is in apposition to "*vous*".

Sometimes the apposition and the qualified word are put directly next to each other, without a comma or a pause:

un enfant **prodige**; *voici mon cousin* **dentiste**
a child prodigy; here is my dentist cousin

⚠ In expressions like:

la ville **de Vancouver**/the town of Vancouver, *le mois* **de juin**/the month of June, *le titre* **de marquis**/the title of Marquis, the words "*Vancouver*", "*juin*" and "*marquis*" are considered as appositions through an indirect structure.

THE NOUN PLACED IN APOSTROPHE

A noun is placed in apostrophe when it indicates a person (or a personified object) who is being called or invoked:

Jeanne, *viens à table!*/Jeanne, come to table!: "*Jeanne*" is placed in apostrophe.

Sonnez, sonnez toujours, **clairons** *de la pensée!* (Victor Hugo): "*clairons*" is placed in apostrophe.

THE NOUN AS ADVERBIAL PHRASE

A noun is an adverbial phrase when it indicates the conditions or circumstances in which the action marked by the verb is accomplished. Adverbial phrases answer the questions: where? when? how? why? how many? etc., when placed after the verb. And so there are adverbial phrases of place, time, manner, etc.

CONSTRUCTION OF ADVERBIAL PHRASES

The adverbial phrase, often introduced by a preposition, can also be constructed directly:

Elle vient cette semaine *à Paris*. Elle marche *avec lenteur*.
She is coming to Paris this week. She walks slowly.

Depuis mardi, je ne l'ai pas vu. Il est parti *mardi*.
I have not seen him since Tuesday. He left on Tuesday.

THE ADVERBIAL PHRASE OF PLACE

● Answers the questions following the verb: *où?* (where?), *d'où?* (from where?), *par où?* (out of where?).
It expresses the meaning of:

– the place where one is: *Il réside à Lyon*.
He lives in Lyons.

– the place where one is going: *Elle se rend à la campagne*.
She is going to the country.

– the place from where one is coming: *Un rat sortit de la terre*.
A rat came out of the ground.

– the place one moves away from: *Elle éloigna la lampe du livre*.
She moved the lamp away from the book.

– the place through which one goes: *Il a sauté par la fenêtre*.
He jumped out of the window.

In a figurative way, it can indicate a person's origin:

Il est issu de famille paysanne./He comes from a peasant family.

● It can be introduced by prepositions, such as:

à: *Il est arrivé à la gare*.
He arrived at the station.

Il puise l'eau à une source.
He draws water from the spring.

chez: *Elle se rend chez son ami*.
She is going to her friend's house.

dans: *Entrez dans la chambre*.
Come into the room.

de: *Elle s'écarte **de la route**.*
She moves away from the road.

sur: *Mettez le livre **sur la table**.*
Put the book on the table.

*Il est né **de parents modestes**.*
He was born of modest parents.

sous: *Cherchez **sous le buffet**.*
Look under the dressser.

par: *Le train passe **par la vallée**.*
The train passes through the valley.

pour: *Elle a pris le train **pour Toronto**.*
She took the train for Toronto.

vers: *Elle marche **vers la voiture**.*
She walks towards the car.

en: *Restez **en classe**.*
Stay in class.

and also ***parmi**/*among (with the plural), ***jusqu'à**/*to, as far as, ***contre**/*against, etc.

⚠ The adverbial phrase can be constructed without a preposition (not to be confused with a direct object):

*Il demeure **rue Victor Hugo**.* (Where does he live?)
He lives in the rue Victor Hugo.

THE ADVERBIAL PHRASE OF TIME

● The adverbial phrase of time answers the questions ***quand?**/*when?, ***combien de temps?**/*how long?, ***depuis combien de temps?**/*since when? It expresses:

– the date of the action: *Je prends mes vacances **en août**.*
I take my holidays in August.

– the time of the action: *Elle est sortie à **cinq heures**.*
She went out at five o'clock.

– the duration of the action: *Il marcha **trente jours**.*
He walked for thirty days.

● It can be introduced by prepositions, such as:

à: *À **l'aube**, la campagne s'anime.*
At daybreak the countryside comes to life.

vers: *Le vent se leva **vers le soir**./*The wind came up towards the evening.

de: *Il est venu **de bonne heure**.*
He came early.

sur: *Elle rentrera **sur les six heures**./*She will be back by six o'clock.

dans: *J'aurai terminé **dans un instant**.*
I'll be finished in a minute.

pour: *Elle est partie **pour deux jours**./*She has left for two days.

en: *La neige est tombée **en janvier**.*
The snow fell in January.

durant: *Je l'ai vu **durant mon voyage**./*I saw him during my trip.

⚠ The adverbial phrase of time can be constructed without a preposition (not to be confused with a direct object): *Il resta **un mois** à l'étranger./*He stayed abroad one month. (How long did he stay?)

41

ADVERBIAL PHRASES OF MANNER, POINT OF VIEW AND COMPARISON

● These adverbial phrases answer the questions **comment?**/how?, **de quelle façon?**/in what way?, **par rapport à qui** or **à quoi?**/in relation to whom or to what?, **de quel point de vue?**/from what point of view?. They express:

– the manner in which the action takes place:

*Elle travaille **avec ardeur**.*/She works with enthusiasm.

– depending on the point of view considered:

*Elle réussit mieux **en mathématiques**.*/She succeeds better in mathematics.

– comparison:

*Il est grand **pour son âge**.*/He is tall for his age.

● They can be introduced by prepositions:

à: *Elle allait **à grands pas**.* She strided along.

avec: *Elle refusa **avec mépris**.* She refused with disdain.

de: *regarder **d'un air distrait*** look in an absent-minded way

sans: *Il le regarda **sans colère**.* He looked at him without anger.

en: *examiner la lettre **en silence*** examine the letter in silence

pour: *Il a bien réussi, **pour un essai**.* For a trial go, he succeeded well.

selon: ***Selon ses dires**, il est innocent.* According to what he says, he is innocent.

● They can be constructed directly: *Elle marchait **la tête haute**.*/She was walking with her head high.

● Adverbial phrases of comparison can be introduced by the conjunctions **comme**/as, like and **que**/than:

*Il conduisait **comme** un fou.* He was driving like a madman.

*Elle est plus grande **que** son frère.* She is taller than her brother.

NOTE : In the last examples, *"fou"* and *"frère"* could be considered as being the subjects of implied verbs: *Il conduisait comme un fou conduirait*/He was driving like a madman would drive; *Elle est plus grande que son frère n'est.*/She is taller than her brother is tall., or, perhaps even more accurately, we could make *"frère"* the adverbial comparative of *"plus grand"*.

ADVERBIAL PHRASES OF PRICE AND MEASURE

● This type of adverbial answers the questions **à quel prix?**/at what price?, **combien?**/how much?. They express:

– price: *Il a payé ce terrain **une forte somme**.* He paid a big price for this piece of land.

– measure: *La piste du stade mesure **quatre cents mètres**.* The track in the stadium is four hundred meters long.

– weight: *Ce paquet pèse **trois kilos.***
This parcel weighs three kilos.

● This type of adverbial can be introduced by prepositions such as:

à: *Le terrain est **à un prix excesssif.***
The price of the piece of land is excessive.

pour: ***Pour cette somme**, je vous le donne.*
For that amount, I will let you have it.

de: *Le thermomètre est descendu **de un degré.***
The thermometer went down by one degree.

⚠ These adverbial phrases can be constructed directly (not to be confused with direct objects):

*Un tableau de maître se vend **plusieurs millions**.* (sells for how much?)
A picture by an Old Master sells for several millions.

ADVERBIAL PHRASES OF ACCOMPANIMENT AND PRIVATION

● These adverbials answer the questions ***accompagné de qui? de quoi? avec qui? avec quoi?**/*accompanied by whom? by what? with whom? with what? They express:

– accompaniment: *Il est parti en vacances **avec sa mère**.*
He went on holiday with his mother.

    *L'appareil est vendu **avec ses accessoires**.*
The machine is sold with its accessories.

– privation: *Elle est venue **sans son frère**.*
She came without her brother.

● They can be introduced by the prepositions:

– **avec**: *Elle se promène **avec son chien**. Elle est partie **avec des amis**.*
She is walking with her dog.   She has left with some friends.

– **sans**: *Il voyage **sans sa femme**.*   *Il vit seul **sans ressources**.*
He is travelling without his wife.   He lives alone without any means of support.

THE ADVERBIAL PHRASE OF MEANS

● This type of adverbial phrase answers the questions coming after the verb: ***au moyen de qui? de quoi? avec qui? avec quoi? par quelle partie?**/*by means of who? of what? in what? with what? by which part? They express:

– the instrument: *Elle écrivit son nom **avec un crayon**.*
She wrote her name with a pencil.

– the material:	*La cheminée est **en marbre**.*
	The mantlepiece is in marble.
– parts of the body:	*Je le pris **par le bras**.*
	I took him by the arm.
– parts of an object:	*Pierre me tira **par la manche**.*
	Pierre pulled me by the sleeve.

These adverbials can be introduced by the prepositions:

à: *Tracez vos lignes **à la règle**.*
Draw your lines with a ruler.

avec: *Il découpa la gravure **avec des ciseaux**.*
He cut out the print with scissors.

de: *Elle le poussa **de l'épaule**.*
She pushed it with her shoulder.

par: *Elle le saisit **par le cou**.*
She grabbed him by the neck.

en: *Le cloison est faite **en carreaux de plâtre**.*
The partition is made of plaster tiles.

THE ADVERBIAL PHRASE OF CAUSE

It answers the questions posed after the verb: ***pourquoi?**/why?, **pour quelle raison?**/for what reason? **sous l'effet de quoi?**/under the effect of what? It expresses:

– the cause (proper meaning):	*Elle est morte **d'un cancer**.*
	She died of cancer.
– the reason for:	*Il est entré **par erreur**.*
	He came in by mistake.

● It can be introduced by the prepositions:

de: *Il resta muet **de surprise**.*/He was left dumb with surprise.

par: *Elle renversa un verre **par inadvertance**.*
She knocked over a glass by accident.

pour: *Il fut félicité **pour son succès**.*
He was congratulated on his success.

THE ADVERBIAL PHRASE OF OPPOSITION

The adverbial phrase of opposition (also called "concession") is introduced by the preposition ***malgré**/despite or the prepositional phrase **en dépit de**/in spite of.
It indicates the cause which is in opposition to the action expressed by the verb:

*Elle sortit **malgré la pluie**.*/She went out in spite of the rain.

***En dépit de sa tristesse**, elle souriait.*
In spite of her unhappiness, she was smiling.

THE ADVERBIAL PHRASE OF PURPOSE OR OF INTEREST

● It answers the questions coming after the verb: ***dans quelle intention?*/**
with what intention? ***au profit de qui?*/**to the benefit of whom? or ***contre qui? contre quoi?*/**against whom? against what? It expresses:

- purpose: *Tout le monde se réunit **pour le cortège**.*
Everybody gathered together for the procession.

- interest: *Elle travaille **pour ses enfants**.*/She works for her children.

- hostility: *Il n'a jamais rien fait **contre ses amis**.*
He never acted against his friends.

● It can be introduced by prepositions such as:

- ***à***: *J'ai volé **à son secours**.*/I rushed to his aid.

- ***pour***: *Prends un savon **pour la toilette**.*/Take some soap to wash with.

- ***dans***: *Elle travaille **dans l'espoir de réussir**.*
She is working in the hope of succeeding.

- ***contre***: *Il a voté **contre cette loi**.*/He voted against this law.

THE POSITION OF ADVERBIAL PHRASES

Adverbial phrases can normally be positioned quite freely within a sentence. They are usually placed after the verb and the object; if there are several adverbial phrases, one usually finishes with the longest one:

> *On devinait sa peur, **en ce moment, sous l'impassibilité du visage**.*/One could see her fear, in that moment, beneath the impassivity of her face.

However, some adverbial phrases, in particular those of place and time, can come before the verb:

> ***Le mardi matin, à huit heures**, elle prit l'avion pour Toronto.*
On Tuesday morning, at eight o'clock, she took the plane for Toronto.

QUALIFYING ADJECTIVES

The qualifying adjective is a variable word, indicating the quality of a person or a thing (designated by a noun or a pronoun). It can change its form according to gender and number; *un gentil garçon*/a nice boy, *de petits villages*/little villages; *cela est inutile*/that is pointless.

FORMING THE FEMININE

In general, the feminine of the adjective is formed by adding an **-e** to the end of the masculine form:

> *un grand bureau → une grande échelle*
> a large office → a large scale

> *un hardi marin → une manœuvre hardie*
> a daring sailor → a daring manoeuvre

NOTE : If the masculine form ends in an **-e**, the adjective does not change in the feminine:

> *un large trottoir → une rue large*
> a wide pavement → a wide street

● If the masculine form ends in **-gu**, the feminine is in **-guë** (with a dieresis over the **-e**):

> *un cri aigu → une pointe aiguë*
> a sharp cry → a sharp point

● If the masculine form ends in **-eau, -ou**, the feminine is in **-elle, -olle**:

> *un beau jouet → une belle gravure*
> a beautiful toy → a beautiful engraving

> *un terrain mou → une chaire molle*
> soft earth → flabby flesh

⚠ *Flou*/blurred, *hindou*/hindu have the feminine form: *floue, hindoue.*

● If the masculine form ends in **-el, -ul**, or a palatized **-l**, the feminine form is **-elle, -ulle, -ille**:

> *un cruel ennemi → une farce cruelle*
> a cruel enemy → a cruel joke

> *un devoir nul → une note nulle*
> useless homework → worthless grade mark

> *un pareil espoir → une vie pareille*
> such a hope → such a life

● If the masculine form ends in **-ien**, **-on**, the feminine takes **-ienne**, **-onne**:

> *un château ancien* → *une bague anc**ienne***
> an old castle → an old ring

> *un bon numéro* → *une **bonne** affaire*
> a good number → good business

● If the masculine ends in **-an**, the feminine takes **-ane**:

> *l'esprit partisan* → *une querelle partis**ane***
> the partisan spirit → a partisan quarrel

⚠ **Paysan** becomes *paysanne* in the feminine:

> *le labeur paysan* → *la vie pays**anne***
> peasant's work → peasant's life

● If the masculine form ends in **-et**, the feminine is **-ette**:

> *un élève muet* → *une douleur mu**ette***
> a silent pupil → silent grief

⚠ The adjectives **complet**/complete, **désuet**/old-fashioned, **discret**/discreet, **incomplet**/incomplete, **indiscret**/indiscreet, **inquiet**/anxious, **replet**/podgy, **secret**/secret all take **-ète** in the feminine:

> *un regard inquiet* → *l'âme inqui**ète***
> a worried look → a troubled spirit

● The masculine adjectives which end in **-ot** have **-ote** in the feminine, except **boulot**/job, **maigriot**/thin, **pâlot**/pale, **sot**/silly, **vieillot**/antiquainted which double the **-t**:

> *un conte idiot* → *une farce idi**ote***
> a silly story → a silly joke

> *un sot conseil* → *une so**tt**e réponse*
> silly advice → silly answer

● The masculine **bas**/low, **épais**/thick, **gros**/fat, **faux**/false, **roux**/red, **las**/weary, **exprès**/on purpose, **métis**/half breed have the feminine in **-sse** or **-esse**:

> *un billet faux* → *une pièce fau**sse***
> a forged banknote → a forged coin

> *un ordre exprès* → *une défense expr**esse***
> an express order → formal defence

● If the masculine form ends in **-er**, then the feminine form is in **-ère**:

> *le dernier mot* → *la derni**ère** page*
> the last word → the last page

> *un air léger* → *une brise lég**ère***
> a light air → a light breeze

● If the masculine ends in **-eux**, **-oux**, **-eur**, the feminine is in **-euse**, **-ouse**, **-euse**:

> *un garçon sérieux* → *une idée séri**euse***
> a serious boy → a serious idea

> *un enfant jaloux* → *une fille jal**ouse***
> a jealous child → a jealous girl

> *un rire trompeur* → *une réponse tromp**euse***
> a deceiving laugh → a deceitful answer

⚠ **Antérieur**/previous, **extérieur**/outward, **intérieur**/inner, **majeur**/major, **meilleur**/better, **mineur**/minor, **postérieur**/posterior, **supérieur**/superior, **ultérieur**/ulterior have a feminine form in **-e**:
un meilleur avis → *une meill**eure** vie*/a better opinion → a better life.

● If the masculine form is in **-teur**, the feminine is usually **-trice**, if the **-t** belongs to the suffix:

> *un nom évocateur* → *une phrase évoca**trice***
> a suggestive name → a suggestive phrase

⚠ The masculine adjectives in **-teur** where the **-t** belongs to the stem (which can be seen in the infinitive of the verb from which the adjective is derived) usually take **-teuse** in the feminine:

> *un enfant menteur* → *une fillette ment**euse*** (the **-t** can be seen in *"mentir"*)/a lying child → a lying little girl

● If the masculine form ends in **-f**, the feminine is in **-ve**:

> *un froid vif* → *une vi**ve** discussion*
> a sharp cold → a lively discussion

IRREGULAR FEMININE FORMS

Some adjectives have an irregular form:

Masculine adjective	Feminine ending	Feminine adjective
blanc; franc	-che	*blanche; franche*
frais; sec		*fraîche; sèche*
doux; tiers	-ce	*douce; tierce*
maître; traître	-esse	*maîtresse; traîtresse*
vengeur; pécheur	-eresse	*vengeresse; pécheresse*
bénin; malin	-gne	*bénigne; maligne*
long	-gue	*longue*
caduc; turc	-que	*caduque; turque*
andalou	-se	*andalouse*
favori; coi	-te	*favorite; coite*
hébreu; vieux	(very irregular)	*hébraïque; vieille*

FORMING THE PLURAL OF ADJECTIVES

In general, the plural of an adjective is formed by adding an **-s** to the singular:

> *un grand cahier → de grand**s** espoirs*
> a large notebook → great hopes

> *une phrase brève → de brève**s** phrases*
> a short sentence → short sentences

NOTE : If the singular ends in **-s** or **-x**, the adjective does not change in the plural:

> *un chat gris → des chats gris* *un faux nez → de faux nez*
> a grey cat → grey cats a false nose → false noses

● If the singular ends in **-al**, then the plural takes **-aux**:

> *un tigre royal → des tigres roy**aux***
> a royal tiger → royal tigers

⚠ – *Banal, bancal, fatal, final, glacial, natal, naval, tonal* have the plural in **-als**:

> *le mot final → les combats fin**als***
> the final word → final combats

– The masculine adjectives *beau, hébreu, jumeau, manceau, nouveau, tourangeau* have a plural ending in **-x**:

> *un beau jouet/*a beautiful toy *→ de beau**x** jouets*

POSITION OF THE ATTRIBUTIVE ADJECTIVE

In principle the attributive adjective (see page 58) can be placed either before or after the noun to which it refers:

> *un magnifique point de vue; un point de vue magnifique/*a wonderful viewpoint: the meaning does not change with the change in position of *"magnifique"*.

⚠ Some adjectives have a different meaning according to whether they are placed in front of or after the noun:

> *un **brave** homme/*a good, simple man
> *un homme **brave**/*a courageous man

In fact, the position of the attributive adjective follows a complicated usage which depends in turn on the rhythm of the sentence and the desire for expressiveness.

Generally speaking, the adjective placed before the noun expresses a quality as belonging to the noun and almost forming a single word with it; placed after the noun, it indicates a quality which distinguishes the person or thing from others having the same name:

> *la **petite** maison; l'armée **américaine***
> The small house; the American army

● The following are often placed before the noun:
– a single syllable adjective qualifying a noun of more than one syllable:
un **long** *trajet*/a long journey;
– an adjective which expresses an affective shade of meaning: *le **malheu-
reux** enfant*/the poor child.

● The following adjectives are usually placed after the noun:
– adjectives of more than one syllable which qualify a noun of one syllable:
*un choix **difficile***/a difficult choice;
– adjectives which express the form, the colour or the belonging to a particular category: *un saladier **rond***/a round salad bowl; *une robe **rouge***/a
red dress; *un fonctionnaire **civil***/a civil servant;
– past participles used as adjectives:*des enfants **gâtés***/spoilt children;
– adjectives followed by a phrase: *un travail **long à exécuter***/work taking
a long time to do.

AGREEMENT OF QUALIFYING ADJECTIVES

Qualifying adjectives which are epithetic, predicative or in apposition (see page 58) agree in gender and number with the noun or nouns to which they refer. Thus if the adjective refers to one noun, it agrees in gender and number with this noun; *une grande ferme*/a big farm, *de grands vases*/large vases (epithet adjectives). *Cette ferme est grande.*/This farm is big. *Ces vases sont grands.*/These vases are large. (predicative adjectives).

AGREEMENT OF THE ADJECTIVE WITH MORE THAN ONE NOUN

● If the qualifying adjective refers to two or more nouns, it agrees in number and gender with the nouns taken as a whole:

> *Pierre et Jean sont gentils.*/Pierre and Jean are kind.

> *L'Amérique et l'Asie sont à peu près égales en superficie.*
> America and Asia are about equal in size.

When the nouns are of different gender, the adjective goes into the masculine plural:

> *À l'équinoxe, le jour et la nuit sont égaux.*
> In the spring equinox, night and day are equal in length.

● If the qualifying adjective refers to two single nouns linked by the conjunction *"ou"*, it sometimes agrees with the nearest noun, sometimes with both:

> *une indifférence ou un parti pris révoltant* (agreement with *"parti pris"*)/indifference or appalling onesidedness

> *une paresse ou négligence scandaleuses* (agreement with the two nouns)/laziness or shocking negligence

● If two or more epithetic adjectives refer to the same noun, expressed once in the plural, the adjectives remain in the singular:

> *les langues anglaise et allemande; les Codes civil et pénal*
> the English and German languages; the civil and penal codes

AGREEMENT OF THE ADJECTIVE WITH A NOUN FOLLOWED BY A COMPLEMENT

● If the epithetic adjective refers to a noun followed by a complement, it agrees in gender and in number with the former or the latter, provided it refers in meaning to both elements:

> *un manteau de laine bleu*/a blue woolen coat or *un manteau de laine bleue*/a coat of blue wool: *"bleu"* refers in meaning to both *"manteau"* and *"laine"*.

In other cases, it only agrees with the noun to which it refers in meaning: *un manteau de laine déchiré*/a torn woolen coat made: *"déchiré"* only refers in meaning to *"manteau"*.

● If the qualifying adjective refers to the expression **une espèce de** or **une sorte de**, it agrees with the complement that follows:

> *Une sorte de fou entra, furieux, faisant de grands gestes.*
> Some kind of raging madman came in, waving his arms about.

> *Je vis une espèce de mendiant assis sur le seuil.*
> I saw a kind of beggar sitting in the doorway.

AGREEMENT OF COMPOUND ADJECTIVES

● If the compound adjective is formed from two adjectives, both adjectives agree in number and gender with the noun to which they refer:

> *un enfant sourd-muet*/a deaf and dumb child (= *sourd* and *muet*) → *des enfants sourds-muets*.

● If the compound adjective is formed from an adjective and an adverb (or from a preposition), the adjective agrees but the adverb and the preposition remain unchanged:

> *un enfant nouveau-né* (= *nouvellement né*)/a new born child → *des enfants nouveau-nés*;

> *l'avant-dernière page*/the last but one page → *les avant-dernières pages*;

> *des pois extra-fins*/fine quality peas;

> *des mots sous-entendus*/ implied words.

NOTE : **Nouveau** agrees when the past participle is taken as a noun: *les nouveaux mariés*/the newly weds, *les nouvelles venues*/the newcomers.

● If the compound adjective is formed from an adjective and an element shortened to **-i** or **-o**, only the adjective agrees:

> *une aventure tragi-comique*/a tragi-comic adventure → *des aventures tragi-comiques*;

> *une monnaie gallo-romaine*/gallo-roman money → *des monnaies gallo-romaines*.

AGREEMENT OF COLOUR ADJECTIVES

Colour adjectives agree in number and gender with the noun to which they refer:

> *le tableau noir; les chaussures noires*
> the blackboard; black shoes

▓▓NON-VARIABLE ADJECTIVES OF COLOUR

● Compound adjectives of colour, that is those which are formed with two adjectives or by an adjective and a noun, remain unchanged:

> *une cravate **bleu foncé**; des gants **bleu roi***
> a dark blue tie; royal blue gloves

● Nouns used as adjectives of colour remain unchanged:

> *un ruban orange*/an orange ribbon (the colour of an orange)
> → *des rubans **orange**;*

> *une robe marron*/a chesnut brown dress (the colour of a chesnut)
> → *des robes **marron**.*

EXCEPTIONS

Écarlate/scarlet, *fauve*/tawny, *incarnat*/crimson, *mauve*/mauve, *pourpre*/purple and *rose*/pink indicating colours, are not considered as nouns and agree:

> *un tissu mauve*/a mauve coloured fabric → *des tissus mauv**es**;*

> *une soie rose*/rose coloured silk → *des soies ros**es**.*

Special cases of form and agreement

● The adjectives *fou, vieux, nouveau, beau* and *mou*, have a special masculine singular before a vowel or a silent **-h**, *fol, vieil, nouvel, bel, mol*:

> *un **mol** oreiller;*   *un **bel** homme;*   *un **bel** enfant*
> a soft pillow;   a good-looking man;   a good-looking child

● A few adjectives only have a masculine form; nez *aquilin*/an aquiline nose, *pied **bot***/club foot, *vinaigre **rosat***/pink coloured vinager, and a few adjectives only have a feminine form: *bouche **bée***/flabbergasted, lost for words.

● The adjective *grand* remains unchanged in feminine compound nouns; *grand-route* (main highway); *grand-mère* (grandmother); à *grand-peine* (with great difficulty). However, the form *des grands-mères* is also used.

● The adjective *fort* remains unchanged in the expression *"se faire fort"*:

> *Elle se fit **fort** de lui faire reconnaître son erreur.*
> She made great efforts to make him recognize his mistake.

● The adjective *feu* (= recently deceased) is invariable when it comes before an article:

> ***feu** la reine* but *la **feue** reine.*

● The adjectives **excepté, passé, supposé, compris, ôté, étant donné, ci-joint, ci-inclus, attendu, vu, approuvé, nu, demi** remain unchanged when they come before the noun; they agree when they come after the noun:

> passé huit heures but huit heures passé**es**
> after eight o'clock

> une dem**i**-heure but une heure et demi**e**
> half an hour

> ci-join**t** deux timbres but les deux timbres ci-joint**s**
> two stamps enclosed

> n**u**-tête but tête nu**e**
> bare-headed

● The adjective which follows the verbal expression **avoir l'air** (to seem), can agree with the word "*air*" or, better, with the subject of the verbal expression:

> Elle a l'air **doux**. or Elle a l'air dou**ce**.
> She seems mild-mannered.

● Adjectives used as adverbs or prepositions remain unchanged:

> Ces roses sentent **bon**. La pluie tombe **dru**.
> These roses smell nice. It is raining heavily.

> **Haut** les mains!; des fleurs **plein** les vases
> Hands up!; vases full of flowers

EXCEPTIONS

Des fleurs fra**î**ches écloses; des yeux grand**s** ouverts; une porte grand**e** ouverte.
Flowers just opened; wide open eyes; wide open door.

DIFFERENT DEGREES OF SIGNIFICATION OF ADJECTIVES

The qualifying adjective can simply express a quality of a person or a thing. In this case the adjective is said to be positive: *Cette porte est étroite.*/This door is narrow. *Le courant est rapide.*/The stream is fast-flowing. In some uses, however, it can establish a degree or comparison between people or between things: these are known as the "degrees of signification".

THE COMPARATIVE

If the person or the thing possesses a quality to a certain degree, either inferior, equal or superior with respect to someone or something of the same kind, the comparative is used:

– the comparative of superiority, formed with the adverb *plus:*

> *Pierre est **plus** prudent que Pauline.*/Pierre is more cautious than Pauline.

– the comparative of equality, formed with the adverb *aussi* (or *si* in negative clauses):

> *Pierre est **aussi** aimable que Pauline; Pierre n'est pas **si** habile que Pauline.*
> Pierre is as likeable as Pauline; Pierre is not as clever as Pauline.

– the comparative of inferiority, formed with the adverb *moins:*

> *Pierre est **moins** vif que Pauline.*/Pierre is less lively than Pauline.

THE RELATIVE SUPERLATIVE

If the person or thing possesses a quality to a greater or lesser degree than all the others of the same kind, then the relative superlative is used:

– the relative superlative of superiority is formed with the adverb *le plus*, *le mieux*:

> *Pauline est **la plus** intelligente des élèves. Jean est **le mieux** logé de nous tous.*
> Pauline is the most intelligent of the students. Jean has the best accomodation of us all.

– the superlative relative of inferiority is formed with the adverb *le moins*:

> *Pauline est **la moins** intelligente des élèves.*/Pauline is the least intelligent of the pupils.

THE ABSOLUTE SUPERLATIVE

If one wishes to express that a person or thing possesses a quality to a very high degree, then the absolute superlative is used:

– an absolute superlative can be formed with an adverb like **très, fort, bien**, etc.:

> Marie est **très** intelligente; Jacques est **fort** désagréable.
> Marie is very intelligent; Jacques is most unpleasant.

– an absolute superlative can be formed with a prefix: **archi-, sur-, extra-, super-, hyper-**:

> une salle **archicomble**; une réputation **surfaite**; des petits pois **extra-fins**
> a packed out room; an overrated reputation; extra quality peas

– an absolute superlative can also be formed with the suffix **-issime**:

> un timbre **rarissime**; un homme **richissime**
> an extremely rare stamp; a fabulously wealthy man

IRREGULAR COMPARATIVES AND SUPERLATIVES

Some comparatives and superlatives are irregular in form:

Positive	Comparative	Relative superlative
bon/good	meilleur/better	le meilleur/the best
petit/small	moindre, plus petit/smaller	le moindre, le plus petit/the smallest
mauvais/bad	pire, plus mauvais/worst	le pire, le plus mauvais/the worst

NOTE : French uses forms coming from Latin words which were comparatives and which have the meaning of an ordinary adjective or a superlative. This is the case for **supérieur, inférieur, intérieur, extérieur, ultérieur, antérieur, postérieur**:

> une situation **inférieure**; du chocolat **supérieur**
> a low or a lower position; a better chocolate (or of superior quality)

USE OF THE ARTICLE
BEFORE THE RELATIVE SUPERLATIVE

● The article is not used before a relative superlative when the latter is preceded by a possessive adjective or the preposition **de**:

> C'est **mon plus beau** costume.   Ce qu'il y a **de plus étonnant**.
> It is my best suit.   What is most surprising.

● When several superlatives refer to the same noun, the article is placed before one of them:

*La nouvelle **la** plus étonnante, **la** plus incroyable qu'on ait apprise.*
The most astonishing, unbelievable piece of news one has ever heard.

● In the expressions ***le plus***, ***le moins***, ***le mieux*** (superlatives of adverbs), the article can remain unchanged before a feminine or plural adjective if different degrees of the same quality in one or several things are being compared:

*C'est le matin que la rose est **le** plus **belle**.*
It is in the morning that a rose is at its most beautiful.

*C'est en été que les orages sont **le** plus fréquent**s**.*
It is during the summer that storms are the most frequent.

● But if one or several persons or things are compared to all others of the same kind, then the article is variable:

*La rose est **la** plus belle des fleurs.*
The rose is the most beautiful of flowers.

*Les questions qui paraissent **les** plus simples.*
The questions which seem the simplest.

● If the adjective is used like an adverb, the article remains unchanged:

*Ce sont ces fleurs qui coûtent **le** plus cher.*
These are the most expensive flowers.

Functions of the qualifying adjective

When it is not used as an adverb (see previous page) or as a noun (for example: *le bleu du ciel*/the blue of the sky), the qualifying adjective can have three functions. It can be used as an epithet, or in apposition in a noun group, or predicatively in a verb group. It can also have a complement.

The epithetic adjective

The qualifying adjective is an epithetic adjective when, placed next to the noun, it indicates a quality and forms like a single unit with the noun:

> une **jeune** informaticienne/a young computer scientist: *"jeune"* is the epithet of *"informaticienne"*.

The epithetic adjective can be introduced, after certain indefinite pronouns, by the preposition **de**:

> Il avait sur son visage quelque chose **de grave**./There was something serious about his face.: *"grave"* is an epithet of *"quelque chose"*.

The adjective in apposition

The qualifying adjective is in apposition when it is placed next to a noun or pronoun indicating a quality; in speech it is separated by a slight pause or by a comma in writing:

> **Jeune**, elle marchait d'un pas vif./Being young, she walked at a brisk pace.: *"jeune"* is in apposition to the subject *"elle"*;

> Je vis certains, **inquiets**, qui s'agitaient./I saw some people, worried and anxious, who were getting restless.: *"inquiets"* is in apposition to the direct object *"certains"*.

The predicative adjective

THE PREDICATE OF A SUBJECT

The qualifying adjective is a predicate of the subject, when, linked to a noun or a pronoun by a verb, it expresses a quality attributed to the subject but does not form a single unit with the subject. We find it in:

– stative verbs: Perrette **était jeune**. /Perrette was young.: *"jeune"* is the predicate of the subject *"Perrette"*;

– certain verbs in the passive voice: *Il **fut rendu prudent** par son accident./* His accident made him more careful. (*"prudent"* is the predicate of the subject *"il"*);
– certains intransitive verbs: *Nous **vivions tranquilles**./*We were living peacefully. (*"tranquille"* is the predicate of the subject *"nous"*).

▬THE PREDICATE OF THE OBJECT

The qualifying adjective is a predicate of an object when it represents a quality which the subject recognizes or attributes to the object.
It is found with the verbs: *faire, rendre, juger, choisir, estimer, déclarer,* etc.:

> *Je le **crois sincère**./*I believe him to be sincere.: *"sincère"* is the predicate of the direct object *"le"*;

> *Il **estime** cet enfant **capable**./*He considers this child to be capable.: *"capable"* is the predicate of the direct object *"enfant"*.

⚠ The adjective used predicatively with the subject or the object can be introduced by the prepositions **en, pour, à, de** and by the conjunction **comme**:

> *Pierre agit **en ingrat**./*Pierre acted like an ungrateful person.: *"ingrat"* is the predicate of the subject *"Pierre"*;

> *Je le considère **comme fou**./*I consider him to be a madman.: *"fou"* is the predicate of the direct object *"le"*.

THE COMPLEMENT OF THE ADJECTIVE

▬THE DETERMINING COMPLEMENT

A noun is a determining complement of an adjective when, placed next to the adjective, it complements its meaning:

> *ce bol plein **de lait**/*this bowl full of milk: *"lait"* is the complement of the adjective *"plein"*.

It can be introduced by the prepositions **de, à, envers, en**, etc.:

> *L'alcool est nuisible **à la santé**./*Alcohol is harmful to the health.: *"santé"* is the complement of the adjective *"nuisible"*.

> *Ne soyons pas indulgents **envers nous-mêmes**./*Let us not be indulgent with ourselves.: *"nous-mêmes"* is the complement of the adjective *"indulgents"*.

> *Elle est loyale **envers ses amis**./*She is loyal with her friends.: *"amis"* is the complement of the adjective *"loyale"*.

> *Elle est forte **en mathématiques**./*She is strong in mathematics.: *"mathématiques"* is the complement of the adjective *"forte"*.

The same word can be the complement of several different adjectives coordinated or juxtaposed together, provided that these different adjectives can have the same construction:

*Il est **heureux** et **fier de son succès**.*/He is pleased and proud of his success.

However, one would say:

*Il est **sensible à vos compliments** et il **en est très fier**.*
He is very touched by your compliments and he is very proud of them.

▬THE COMPLEMENTS OF THE COMPARATIVE AND OF THE SUPERLATIVE

An adjective in the comparative or in the relative superlative is usually followed by a complement:

*On a souvent besoin d'un **plus petit** que **soi**.* (La Fontaine)/One often needs lesser people than oneself.: *"soi"* is the complement of the comparative *"plus petit"*.

*L'absence est **le plus grand** des **maux**.* (La Fontaine)/Absence is the greatest of all misfortunes.: *"maux"* is the complement of the superlative *"le plus grand"*.

DETERMINERS OF THE NOUN AND PRONOUNS

The determiner is one of the elements of the noun group. It can belong to different grammatical categories, but it is nearly always associated with the noun. Pronouns are normally used to replace a noun group or to indicate the people who participate in the communication. There are relationships between the determiners and certain pronouns.

DETERMINERS OF THE NOUN

As a general rule, a noun is used preceded by a short word like *le, un, ce,* etc., which is known as the "determiner". Its role is to define the noun and make its meaning clearer.
There are six classes of determiners:

– articles: *le, un, du,* etc.;
– demonstratives: *ce, cette,* etc.;
– possessives: *mon, ton, son,* etc.;
– interrogative and exclamative: *quel;*
– numerals: *deux, trois, quatre,* etc.;
– indefinites: *quelques, chaque, plusieurs,* etc.

ABSENCE OF DETERMINER

In certain cases the determiner is not expressed:

– with certain proper nouns: *Marie, Paul, Marseille;*
– in certain expressions: *faire **attention**/*be careful, *prendre **racine**/*take root;
– with appositions or predicated nouns: *Louis XIV, **roi** de France/*Louis the XIVth king of France; *Son frère est **médecin**./*His brother is a doctor.;
– with noun complements preceded by a preposition: *un collier de **perles**/*a pearl necklace; *arriver en **voiture**/*to arrive by car;
– in proverbs and formal expressions: ***Comparaison** n'est pas raison./* Comparisons are odious.

PRONOUNS

Pronouns function as noun groups, substituting for the nouns in order to recall them, to make clearer or to anticipate them, etc. They have all the syntactical functions of a noun.

Among the different pronouns we can distinguish:
- personal pronouns: *il, elle, eux, se, le, la, lui*, etc.;
- possessive pronouns: *le mien, le tien, le sien*, etc.;
- demonstrative pronouns: *ce, ceci, cela, ceux-ci*, etc.;
- relative pronouns: *qui, que, lequel*, etc.;
- indefinite pronouns: *aucun, nul, chacun*, etc.

SIMILARITIES
BETWEEN DETERMINERS AND PRONOUNS

Pronouns show some similarities with determiners:
- pronouns and indefinite adjectives have similar forms:

  aucun, nul, quelque, certain, etc.:

- possessive pronouns and adjectives, demonstrative pronouns and adjectives are closely related by their forms:

  notre (adjective = determiner)/*le nôtre* (pronoun); *mien* (adjective = determiner)/*le mien* (pronoun);

  ce can be either a determiner or a pronoun;

- personal pronouns and articles sometimes have the same form: *le, la, les*.

These similarities highlight the close relationship between the noun group, having a determiner, and the pronoun, substituting for a noun group.

THE ARTICLE

The article is the most commonly used of all the determiners. It is a short variable word which goes with the noun, indicates the gender and number and determines it more precisely. We distinguish three types of articles: the definite article, the indefinite article and the partitive article.

FORMS OF THE ARTICLE

The article can take three forms: normal, elided and contracted.
The elided forms are used before singular words beginning with a vowel or a silent **h-**. The contracted forms are the result of a contraction of the prepositions **de** and **à** and the definite article **le** and **les**.

Article	Singular		Plural	
	Masculine	Feminine	Masculine	Feminine
normal definite	*le* monde	*la* terre	*les* astres	*les* planètes
elided definite	*l'*univers *l'*horizon	*l'*aurore *l'*habilité		
contracted definite	*au* monde (à + le) *du* monde (de + le)	*à la* terre *de la* terre	*aux* hommes (à + les) *des* cieux (de + les)	*aux* femmes (à + les) *des* femmes (de + les)
indefinite	*un* monde	*une* terre	*des* mondes	*des* terres
partitive	boire *du* thé	boire *de la* tisane	manger *des* épinards	manger *des* confitures

When two or more nouns are coordinated, the article is repeated in front of each noun:

> On apercevait *les* toits et *les* cheminées des premières maisons.
> We could make out the roof tops and chimneys of the first houses.

EXCEPTIONS

The article is not repeated:

– in some ready-made expressions: *les* us et coutumes/the habits and customs; *les* pertes et profits/profit and loss;

– when the two nouns are coordinated by an explanatory *ou*/or: *les* Trifluviens, *ou* habitants de Trois-Rivières/the Trifluvians, or inhabitants of Three Rivers.

THE DEFINITE ARTICLE AND ITS USES

● The definite article determines precisely the noun that it introduces:

Répétez la phrase que vous venez de lire./Repeat the sentence you have just read. (*"la"* determines the noun *"phrase"*, indicating it is the one you have just read).

It can also have the meaning of:

– a demonstrative adjective: *J'arrive à l'instant.*/I'm just coming. (= this instant);

– a possessive adjective: *J'ai mal à la tête.*/I've got a headache. (= in my head);

– an indefinite adjective: *tissu à vingt francs le mètre*/fabric at twenty francs a metre (= each metre).

● The definite article is not expressed in front of proper nouns of individual people or towns, unless these names include the article (ex: *La Rochelle*), but it is used in front of the names of different peoples, countries and rivers:

Duval, Québec, Genève but *les Américains, le Mexique, la Seine.*

However, the article is used in front of names indicating:

– families:	*les Valois; les Bourbons*
– the name of a person accompanied by an adjective:	*l'odieux Tarfuffe; le pauvre Pierre*
– the names of despised people:	*la Du Barry; la Brinvilliers*
– the names of admired people:	*les Corneille; les Sévigné*
– artists (of former times):	*la Champmeslé; la Callas*

● The definite article, like other determiners, can be omitted in the following cases:

– names in apposition:	*Ottawa, capitale du Canada*/Ottawa, capital of Canada
– complements of material:	*une statue de marbre*/a marble statue
– verbal expressions:	*Il prit soin de lui.*/He took care of him.
– ready-made expressions:	*Elle est nu-pieds.*/She is barefooted. *à vol d'oiseau*/as the crow flies
– proverbs:	*À bon chat, bon rat.*/Tit for tat.
– addresses:	*Elle habite rue Victor Hugo.*/She lives in the rue Victor Hugo.
– book titles:	*Histoire de France*/The History of France
– enumeration:	*Femmes, moine, vieillards, tout était descendu.* (La Fontaine)/The women, the monk, the old people, all had come down.

The names of countries in the feminine, do not take the article when they are preceded by the prepositions **à**, **de**, **en**:

Elle habite **à** Chypre./She lives in Cyprus.
Elle revient **de** Tunisie./She has come back from Tunisia.
Elles vont **en** Chine./They are going to China.

THE INDEFINITE ARTICLE AND ITS USES

● The indefinite article introduces a name, showing it to be distinct from others of the same kind, without giving any further details.
In the plural it indicates an indefinite number of something:

Un homme est là qui vous attend./There is a man waiting for you there.
Il y a **des** cerises cette année./There are plenty of cherries this year.

The indefinite article can also have the values of:

– the indefinite adjective **quelque**: On le crut pendant **un** temps./For some time it was believed;
– contempt, respect: Les critiques d'**un** Durand ne me troublent pas./Criticisms from someone like Durand don't bother me. Écoutez la prière d'**une** mère./Listen to the prayers of a mother.

● The indefinite article is omitted in front of:
– a noun predicate (sometimes):   Elle devint ingénieur./She became an engineer.
– a noun constructed with
a preposition (sometimes):   Elle est partie en voiture./She left by car.
par endroits/in places
– impersonal expressions: C'est dommage./It's a pity.
– in verbal expressions: faire grâce/to favour
avoir recours à/to resort to

● Often, the article is not expressed after the prepositions **avec** or **sans**, especially with abstract nouns:

Il travaille **avec** peine./He works with great effort.
Elles trouvèrent **sans** difficulté./They found it without difficulty.

THE PARTITIVE ARTICLE AND ITS USES

● The partitive article is used in front of nouns to indicate an indeterminate quantity:

Il boit **du** jus de fruit./He drinks fruit juice.
Il vend **de la** soie./He sells silk.
Elle mange **des** confitures./She eats jam.

⚠ **Des** rarely has partitive meaning, since it is generally used as an indefinite article (plural of **un**).

● The preposition **de** is used alone, in place of a partitive or an idefinite article, in the following cases:

– after an adverb of quantity time (*trop, peu, beaucoup*, etc.): *J'ai **peu de** temps devant moi.*/I have little time left.
*J'ai **trop de** travail.*/I have too much work.

except in **bien des**: ***Bien des** gens disent…*/Many people say… (**des** is a partitive article here.)

– after a verb in the negative: *Elle ne boit pas **de** lait.*/She doesn't drink milk.

– in front of a plural noun preceded by an adjective: *Elle nous a servi **de beaux** fruits.*/She served us with gorgeous fruit.

Numerals

The numerical adjectives, or numerals, indicate the number or exact rank of the persons or the things they determine or qualify. The cardinal numerals express a precise numerical quantity (*une ville de trois cent mille habitants*/a town with three hundred thousand inhabitants). The ordinal numerals express an exact rank in a sequence (*Elle habite au troisième étage.*/She lives on the third floor.).

Forms of Numerals

CARDINALS

The cardinal numerals can have the following forms:

– single words: *un, deux, trois, quatre, quatorze, quinze, trente, cent, mille*, etc.;
– compound words, either by addition (*dix-huit, vingt et un*); or by multiplication (*quatre-vingts; deux cents*).

The normal usage is to place a hyphen in the compound numerals under one hundred which are not linked by the conjunction *et*:

> *Vingt-deux*/twenty two but *vingt et un*/twenty one, *trois cents*/three hundred.

ORDINALS

The ordinals are as follows:

– words formed with the suffix **-ième** with single or compound cardinals: *troisième, millième; vingt et unième, trente-deuxième, trois centième* (the **-ième** suffix is only added to the last of the adjectives);
– individual words: *premier, second*.

⚠ Ordinal numerals have the role of qualifying adjectives; they are not determiners, so they are usually used with an article, a demonstrative or a possessive, etc.:

> *C'est la **première** fois que je la vois.*/It's the first time I have seen her.

> *Donne-lui une **deuxième** chance.*/Give him a second chance.

Agreement of Numerals

CARDINALS

The cardinal numerals are invariable:

> ***trente-quatre** lignes*/thirty four lines; *page **cent huit***/page one hundred and eight; ***deux mille** soldats*/two thousand soldiers.

EXCEPTIONS

– **un** becomes **une** in the feminine; *vingt et* **une** *pages*/twenty one pages;
– **vingt** and **cent** take the plural form in those cases where they are multiplied by another numeral and form the second part of a numerical adjective:

> *deux cents*/two hundred; *quatre-vingts*/eighty;

but one does not normally put an **-s** if they are followed by another numeral: *deux cent* **un**/two hundred and one; *quatre-vingt-***deux**/eighty two.

ORDINALS

The ordinal numerals vary in number and gender with the noun they refer to: *les premières pages d'un livre*/the first pages of a book.

SPECIAL USES

● The cardinal numeral is often used with ordinal meaning (in this case it is always invariable) to indicate:
– the day, the time, the year:

> *le quinze janvier mille neuf cent deux* à *huit heures*/the fifteenth of January nineteen hundred and two at eight o'clock (the thousands are sometimes written as **mil**: *mil neuf cent*);

– the title of a sovereign or of a prince:

> *Charles* **huit** (usually written in roman numerals *Charles VIII*/Charles the eighth), but one says: *François* **premier** (written François Ier);

– the number of a house, or a page:

> *au* **trente**, *rue Mozart*/thirty rue Mozart; *page* **quatre-vingt**/page eighty.

● The cardinal or ordinal numeral can indicate an imprecise or symbolic quantity:

> *Attendez* **deux** *minutes.*/Wait a minute. *C'est la centième fois que je te le dis!*/I have told you that a hundred times!

NUMERICAL NOUNS

The numerical nouns are:
– numerals used as nouns:

> **Deux** *et* **deux** *font* **quatre**.*/Two and two make four.

> *Je ne répéterai pas le* **centième** *de ce qu'il m'a dit.*/I won't repeat a hundredth part of what he told me.

– multiplier nouns used as qualifying adjectives:

le **double**/double, le **triple**/triple, un **triple saut**/a triple jump, une **double page**/a double page

– nouns formed with the suffix **-aine** indicating a more or less precise quantity:

une **vingtaine** de badauds/around twenty onlookers; une **douzaine** d'œufs/a dozen eggs

– nouns formed with the suffix **-ain** indicating the number of verses in a stanza:

Un sonnet comprend deux **quatrains** et deux tercets.
A sonnet has two quatrains and two triplets.

– nouns indicating a fraction:

Payez le **tiers** de vos impôts./Pay the third of your taxes.

POSSESSIVE ADJECTIVES AND PRONOUNS

The possessive adjectives indicate that a person or a thing belongs to someone or something. Their function is therefore to relate to the person or thing "possessed" with which they agree: *Il a vendu sa maison.*/He has sold his house. (= the house which belonged to him, *"sa"* is feminine like *"maison"*). The possessive pronouns stand for a noun, but add the idea of possession, with reference to a person or a thing: *Mon devoir d'algèbre est plus difficile que le tien.*/My algebra homework is more difficult than yours. (*le tien* = your homework).

FORMS OF POSSESSIVE ADJECTIVES

Possessive adjectives vary according to gender and number of the thing or the person "possessed" and with the person or the "possessor":

J'apporte mon livre./I bring my book. (1st person)

Elles apportent leurs livres./They bring their books. (3rd person)

	One possessor		More than one possessor	
Person and gender	A thing or person	Several things or persons	A thing or person	Several things or persons
1st pers.masc.	mon livre	mes livres	notre livre	nos livres
fem.	ma chienne	mes chiennes	notre chienne	nos chiennes
2nd pers. masc.	ton livre	tes livres	votre livre	vos livres
fem.	ta chienne	tes chiennes	votre chienne	vos chiennes
3rd pers. masc.	son livre	ses livres	leur livre	leurs livres
fem.	sa chienne	ses chiennes	leur chienne	leurs chiennes

⚠ When there is a vowel or a silent **h-** at the beginning of a feminine noun, **mon, ton, son** are used instead of *"ma", "ta", "sa"*:

Sa grand fille me renseigna. → *Son aimable fille me renseigna.*
His grown-up daughter informed me. → His kind daughter informed me.

NOTE: The forms **mien, tien, sien, nôtre, leur,** are sometimes used as epithets or predicatively with a subject or an object:

Cette opinion est mienne./This opinion is mine.

Ils ont déclaré faire leurs ces revendications./They declared they would make these demands theirs.

MEANING OF POSSESSIVE ADJECTIVES

The possessive adjectives can indicate:

– possession: **Mes** cahiers sont sur mon bureau./My exercise books are on the table.;

– origin: **Mon** pays est là-bas près de la mer./My country is down there near the sea.;

– subject of the action: **Sa** faute est de ne pas avouer./His mistake is not confessing.;

– object of the action: À **ma** vue elle se tait (en me voyant)./She falls silent on seeing me.;

– repetition, habit: Elle a raté **son** train./She missed her train.; Prenez-vous **votre** café?/Are you going to drink your coffee?

– affection, interest: **Notre** Jean-Claude est tout heureux./Our Jean-Claude is very happy.;

SPECIAL CASES OF POSSESSIVE ADJECTIVES

● The possessive adjective is replaced by the definite article when it concerns parts of the body or clothing and the possessor is clearly indicated:

Elle a levé **le** bras. Il a mal à **la** tête. Il le saisit par **la** ceinture.

She raised her arm. He's got a headache. He grabbed him by the belt.

● When the possessor is the indefinite pronoun **on**, the possessive adjective is **son, sa, ses**. When "on" means **nous**, the possessive adjective is **notre, nos** (familiar style).

On a droit d'avoir **son** opinion.
One has the right to one's opinion.

On ne voit plus **nos** amies.
We don't see our friends anymore.

● When the possessor is the indefinite pronoun **chacun**, the possessive adjective is normally **son, sa, ses**, but it can aslo be **leur** or **leurs** when chacun is preceded by a plural noun:

Chacun tenait **son** livre.   Les élèves ont chacun **leur** crayon.
Each one had his book.   Each student has his pencil.

● The possessive adjective can be replaced by the personal pronoun **en** when the possessor is the name of a thing and is not in the same clause as the possessed thing:

La **maison** était fermée, mais j'**en** avais les clefs (= the keys of the house).
The house was locked up, but I had the keys.

FORMS AND FUNCTIONS OF POSSESSIVE PRONOUNS

● The possessive pronouns are formed in using the definite article and a possessive adjective. They vary in gender, in number and in person.

Person and gender	One possessor		Several possessors	
	A thing or person	More than one thing or person	A thing or person	More than one thing or person
1st pers. masc. fem.	*le mien* *la mienne*	*les miens* *les miennes*	*le nôtre* *la nôtre*	*les nôtres* *les nôtres*
2nd pers. masc. fem.	*le tien* *la tienne*	*les tiens* *les tiennes*	*le vôtre* *la vôtre*	*les vôtres* *les vôtres*
3rd pers. masc. fem.	*le sien* *la sienne*	*les siens* *les siennes*	*le leur* *la leur*	*les leurs* *les leurs*

● Like all pronouns, possessive pronouns can function as nouns:

Je ne trouve pas ta brosse à dent; je ne vois que la mienne (= my toothbrush).

                                                                                                          direct object of "*vois*"

I can't find your toothbrush, I can only see mine.

DEMONSTRATIVE ADJECTIVES AND PRONOUNS

Demonstrative adjectives, which are more accurately referred to as demonstrative determiners, meaning "this/these" and "that/those" in English, are used to designate persons or things: *Cette pendule retarde.*/This clock is slow. De-

monstrative pronouns represent a noun group. They take it up again and refer to it precisely: *Je voudrais changer d'appartement car celui-ci est trop petit.*/I would like to move to another flat because this one is too small.

FORMS OF DEMONSTRATIVE ADJECTIVES

Demonstrative adjectives agree in gender and number with the noun they refer to and which they determine: *La foudre a frappé ce grand chêne.*/Lightning has struck this big oak tree.
They are of simple form or reinforced form.

● The simple forms are shown in the following table:

Number	Masculine	Feminine
singular simple form	*ce mur; ce hérisson* (before consonant or aspirated h-) *cet arbre; cet homme* (before vowel or silent h-)	*cette ardeur* *cette histoire* *cette honte*
plural simple form	*ces murs* *ces héros*	*ces tables* *ces huîtres*

● The reinforced forms are constructed with the adverbs of place *ci* and *là*, placed after the noun, and linked to it by a hyphen.
Ci indicates nearness: *cette voiture-ci*; *ce lieu-ci*; *cet arbre-ci*.
Là usually indicates distance. It is mostly used as a single particle to reinforce the demonstrative, without any particular meaning: *cet arbre-là*/that tree there; *ce livre-là*/that book there.

NOTE: When used together, the two reinforced forms can distinguish between two different objects: *Je prendrai ce bracelet-ci et cette montre-là.*/I will take this bracelet and that watch.

Uses of demonstrative adjectives

Demonstrative adjectives can also indicate:

– the person or thing one is going to speak about or that one has just spoken about:

> *Il n'avait guère le temps, disait-il. **Cette** réponse ne satisfit personne.*
> He hardly had the time, he said. This reply satisfied nobody.

– the period of time one is living in or the present circumstances:

> ***Cette** année, l'hiver a été rude. J'ai été malade **ce** mois-**ci**.*
> This year the winter has been hard. I have been ill this month.

– contempt (perjorative use):

> *Que me veut **cet** individu?*
> What does this person want from me?

– admiration (laudatory use):

> *Mon père, **ce** héros au sourire si doux...* (Victor Hugo)
> My father, that hero with such a gentle smile...

– astonishment or indignation:

> *Tu me demandes si j'accepte? **Cette** question!*
> You are asking me if I accept? What a question that is!

Forms of demonstrative pronouns

Like the demonstrative adjectives, the demonstrative pronouns are of simple form or are reinforced by the adverbs *-ci* and *-là*.
The elided form *c'* is mostly used with the forms of the verb "*être*" which begin with a vowel.

Number	Masculine	Feminine	Neuter
simple singular	*celui*	*celle*	*ce/c'*
reinforced sing.	*celui-ci; celui-là*	*celle-ci; celle-là*	*ceci; cela; ça*
simple plural	*ceux*	*celles*	
reinforced plur.	*ceux-ci; ceux-là*	*celles-ci; celles-là*	

NOTES :

1. Like the adjective determiners, the reinforced forms indicate nearness (*ci*) or distance (*là*), or distinguish between two things or persons: *Choisisez une cravate; **celle-ci** est fort jolie; **celle-là** est plus simple.*/Choose a tie; this one is very pretty; that one is plainer. Notice that English frequently uses "this one, that one", but in French "*celle-ci, celle-là*" are all that are required.

2. The neuter demonstrative pronouns indicate a thing, an idea, a quality. They can also represent a clause or an adjective: *Je partirai la semaine prochaine pour Zurich; **cela** est décidé depuis longtemps.*/I am leaving for Zurich next week, that was decided a long time ago.

3. The form ***ça*** is used in familiar speech.

Uses of demonstrative pronouns

● The simple forms ***celui, celle, ceux*** and ***celles*** are never used by themselves; they must be accompanied by a noun complement or a relative pronoun:

> *Il a dépensé toutes ses économies et **celles de son ami**.*
> He has spent all his savings and those of his friend.

> *Elle a remercié **ceux qui** avaient rendu service.*
> She thanked all those who had helped her.

● The reinforced forms and the neuter pronoun ***ce*** can be used alone, without complement or relative:

> *Prenez donc **celui-ci!***
> Take this one!

> ***Ce** serait un scandale.*
> That would be a scandal.

> *Sur **ce**, je vous quitte.*
> On that (note), I leave you.

THE NEUTER PRONOUN "CE"

● The neuter pronoun ***ce*** is used as the subject of the verb *"être"* or as an antecedent of a relative:

> *Il pleut, **c'**est bon pour les plantes.*
> It's raining, that's good for the plants.

> *C'est **ce** que je voulais vous dire.*
> That is what I wanted to tell you.

⚠ One should not confuse ***ce***, the antecedent of a relative, with ***ce que*** which introduces an indirect question:

> *Dis-moi **ce que** tu veux.*/Tell me what you want.

● The neuter pronoun ***ce*** forms a demonstrative expression with the verb *"être"*, where the verb can agree with the real subject ("ce" being the apparent subject):

> ***Ce sont*** or ***c'est** des faux-billets.*/These are forged notes.

> ***Ce sont** eux* or ***c'est** eux.*/It's them.

75

Agreement in the plural is more common in the written language or in formal speech, than in familiar speech.

⚠ One should not confuse **ce** as apparent subject and **ce** as real subject:

> C'est bien la route ./This is the right road.
>
> real subject   predicate of
>   the subject "c'"

*C'est un plaisir de l'**entendre**.*/It's a pleasure to hear him.: "c'" is the apparent subject, "*entendre*" is the real subject (= *l'entendre est un plaisir*).

● The structure *c'est* followed by one of the relative pronoun forms or the conjunction *que* is used to form the typically French expressions *c'est... qui, c'est... que*, which by their cleft structure highlight a word or a group of words:

*C'est Jeanne **qui** a gagné. C'est* (or *ce sont*) *elles **qui** se trompent.*
It's Jeanne who won. It's they who are wrong.

*C'est sérieusement **que** je vous le propose.*
It is seriously that I am proposing it to you.

*C'est parce que j'étais dans mon tort **que** je n'ai rien répondu.*
It was because I was in the wrong that I did not reply.

FUNCTIONS OF DEMONSTRATIVE PRONOUNS

Like any pronoun, the demonstrative pronoun has all the functions of the noun:

– subject: *Celui qui donnera un renseignement sur le disparu sera récompensé*. ("*celui*" is the subject of "*sera récompensé*")/Anybody giving information about the missing person will be rewarded.;

– predicate: *Ses sentiments n'étaient pas **ceux** d'un ingrat*. ("*ceux*" is the predicate of the subject "*sentiments*")/His feelings were not those of an ungrateful person.;

– direct object: *Elle regarda longuement **celui** qui s'avançait*. ("*celui*". is the direct object of "*regarda*")/She took a long look at the one who was coming towards her.;

– predicative indirect object: *Je laisse ce soin à **celles** qui suivront*. ("*celles*" is the predicative indirect object of "*laisse*")/I will leave that responsibility to those following later.;

– adverbial complement or agent: *J'ai été retenu par **celui** dont je t'avais parlé*. ("*celui*" is the agent of "*ai été retenu*")/I was kept back by the one I was telling you about.;

– noun complement: *J'ignore la cause de tout **ceci**.* ("*ceci*" is the complement of the noun "*cause*")/I do not know the cause of all this.;

– adjectival complement: *Ce malheur est-il comparable à **celui** qu'a provoqué l'inondation?* ("*celui*" is the complement of the adjective "*comparable*")/This misfortune, is it comparable to that caused by the flooding?

PERSONAL PRONOUNS

Personal pronouns designate who is speaking (1ˢᵗ person: *je reçois/*I receive), to whom one is speaking (2ⁿᵈ person: *vous recevez/*you receive); and about whom or what one is speaking (3ʳᵈ person: *elle reçoit/*she receives, *ils reçoivent/*they receive).

GENDER OF PERSONAL PRONOUNS

Personal pronouns can be either masculine or feminine, like the nouns they represent: but only the 3ʳᵈ person has different forms in the masculine and feminine:

Il répond (masculine). → *Elle* répond (feminine).
He answers. → She answers.

Je suis surpris (masculine). → *Je* suis surprise (feminine).
I am surprised. → I am surprised.

NOTES :

1. The 3ʳᵈ person pronoun can replace a noun which has already been expressed:

Le voyageur ouvrit son portefeuille, *il* chercha quelques instants et tendit son ticket. ("*il*" represents "*le voyageur*")/The traveller opened his wallet, looked in it a moment and handed over his ticket.

2. The 3ʳᵈ person pronoun can be of neuter gender when it replaces an adjective or a whole clause:

Êtes-vous courageux? Je *le* suis./Are you brave? I am. ("*le*" represents "*courageux*"; "*le*" is neuter);

Il est nécessaire que vous partiez./You will have to leave. ("*il*" replaces "*que vous partiez*"; "*il*" is neuter).

FORMS OF PERSONAL PRONOUNS

The forms of the personal pronoun, which are variable in gender and number, can be unaccented (or "unstressed"), when they simply represent the person and they are attached to the verb. These are known as conjunctive pronouns:

Je ne discuterai pas./I will not argue. ("*Je*" is unstressed).

The personal pronouns are accented (or "stressed"), when they serve to highlight the person.

These are known as disjunctive pronouns:

Moi, *je ne discuterai pas.* /I, personally, will not argue. (*"moi"* is stressed).

NOTE : The stressed personal pronoun can be reinforced by *"même"*:

Toi-même, *tu t'y refuserais.* /You, yourself, would refuse.

	Singular		Plural	
Person	**Unstressed**	**Stressed**	**Unstressed**	**Stressed**
1st person	*je, me*	*moi*	*nous*	*nous*
2nd person	*tu, te*	*toi*	*vous*	*vous*
3rd person	*il, elle* *le, la, lui, en, y*	*lui, elle*	*ils, elles* *les, leur, en, y*	*eux, elles*
reflexive	*se*	*soi*	*se*	

⚠ The personal pronoun can have elided forms: **l'**, **m'**, **t'**, **j'** for **le**, **la**, **me**, **te**, **je** before a vowel or a silent -h in the word following:

*Tu **t'**ennuies.*	*Il **m'**appelle.*	*J'habite Bruxelles.*
You are bored.	He calls me.	I live in Brussels.

FUNCTIONS OF PERSONAL PRONOUNS

Personal pronouns can have the functions of a noun. Only the stressed forms can be attributive.

Functions	Unstressed forms	Stressed forms
subject	*Je comprends son émotion.* *Tu ne m'as rien dit.* *Il n'a pas entendu.* *Elle n'est pas venue.* *Ils sont partis.*	*Moi, j'agirai autrement.* *Toi, tu as oublié.* *Lui, il n'en a rien su.* *Elle, elle ne m'a pas vu.* *Eux, ils ne t'ont pas cru.*
attribute		*C'est **moi** qui lui ai parlé.* *C'est **elle** qui est venue.*
direct object	*Je t'estime beaucoup.* *Je **le** crois sur parole.* *Elle **vous** appelait.*	*Elle t'a invité, **toi**.* *Je le crois, **lui**.* *Félicitez-**vous**.*
indirect object	*Il **lui** en a beaucoup voulu.*	*À **elle**, tu as toujours obéi.*
adverbial phrase	*Elle n'**en** dort plus.*	*Je suis arrivé après **eux**.*

THE NEUTER PRONOUNS "IL" AND "LE"

The neuter *il* pronoun introduces an impersonal verb or announces the real subject of a verb, whose apparent subject is *il*:

Il pleut.	*Il* vous arrivera malheur.	
impersonal verb	apparent subject	real subject
It's raining.	You will have a misfortune.	

● The neuter pronoun *le* (with the meaning of *"cela"*) refers to a masculine or feminine adjective, either singular or plural, or to a clause which precedes it:

*Êtes-vous satisfaite? Je le suis (= je suis satisfaite)./*Are you satisfied? I am.

*Courageux, ils le sont (= ils sont courageux)./*Courageous, they are.

*Elle est plus intelligente que tu ne le penses (= que tu ne penses qu'elle est intelligente)./*She is more intelligent than you think.

USES OF "NOUS" AND "VOUS"

● *Nous* is used for *"je"* in official style, in order to give greater authority to what is said; this is sometimes referred to as the "royal we":

*Nous, maire, ordonnons qu'à dater de.../*We, Mayor, command that as from…

● *Nous* is used instead of *"tu"* to indicate affection or the interest one has for a particular person: this is known as the "affectionate we":

*Avons-nous bien dormi, mon garçon?/*Did we sleep well, my boy?

● *Vous* is used instead of *"tu"* to show respect; this is the polite *vous*. *Tu* indicates familiarity:

*Vous disiez, Monsieur?/*You were saying, sir? (polite *vous*);

*Tu m'ennuies!/*You're bothering me! (familiar *tu*).

⚠ In the examples given below, if the adjective or the participle refers to a plural pronoun indicating a single person, it agrees in the singular and the gender of the person in question:

– "royal we": *Nous, président... sommes saisi d'une demande de.../*We, president… have been submitted a request…

– "affectionate we": *Sommes-nous bien rétablie, Anne?/*Are we better now, Anne?

– "polite vous": *Vous êtes bien pressée, Jeanne!/*You're quite in a hurry, Jeanne!

THE REFLEXIVE PERSONAL PRONOUN

There is a reflexive form of the personal pronoun; it is only used as a complement and indicates the subject who carries out the action on himself:

*Je **me** lave.*
I wash myself.

*Elle **se** lave.*
She washes herself.

*Nous **nous** lavons.*
We wash ourselves.

*Elles **se** lavent.*
They wash themselves.

The reflexive pronoun only has special forms in the 3rd person (*se, soi*); in the other persons it has the form of a pronoun complement:

*Il **se** lave.*
He washes himself.

*Elle **se** lave.*
She washes herself.

*Tu **te** laves.*
You wash yourself.

*Vous **vous** lavez.*
You wash yourself.

The reflexive pronoun **soi** is mostly used to refer to an indeterminate subject (**personne, chacun, on, celui, qui, plus d'un**, etc.):

*Chacun pense à **soi**, avant de penser aux autres.*
Everybody thinks of himself, before thinking of others.

THE PERSONAL PRONOUN "EN"

The invariable personal pronoun **en**, is the equivalent of **de lui, d'elle, d'eux, de cela** (neuter) and can have the following functions:

– noun complement: *La vivacité de son esprit est grande; elle nous **en** cache parfois la profondeur.*/She has a great liveliness of mind; she sometimes hides its depth. "*en*" is here the complement of the noun "*profondeur*" (the depth of her mind);

– adjective complement: *Elle a réussi et elle **en** est fière.*/She has succeeded and she is very proud of the fact.: "*en*" here is the adjective complement of "*fière*" (*fière de sa réussite*);

– direct object: *Avez-vous envoyé des lettres? Je n'**en** ai pas reçu.*/Have you sent any letters? I haven't receive any.: "*en*" is the direct object of "*ai reçu*" (*Je n'ai pas reçu de lettres*);

– indirect object: *Vous m'avez rendu service et je m'**en** souviendrai.*/You helped me and I will remember that.: "*en*" is the indirect object of "*souviendrai*" (*je me souviendrai de cela*);

– adverbial phrase of cause: *Elle a eu la grippe.; elle **en** est restée très affaiblie.*/She has had the flu and it has left her very weakened.: "*en*" is the adverbial phrase of cause of "*affaiblie*" (*affaiblie à cause de cette grippe*);

– adverbial phrase of means: *Il prit une pierre et l'**en** frappa.*/He took a stone and hit him with it.: "*en*" here is the adverbial phrase of means of "*frappa*" (*il le frappa avec cette pierre*).

The pronoun **en** is mainly used to replace inanimate object nouns. To refer to animate objects, the variable personal pronoun is preferred; *lui, elle, eux, elles*, etc.:

*Avez-vous lu son livre? Il est facile de s'**en** souvenir.*
Have you read his book? It is easy to remember it.

*L'avez-vous connu? Il est facile de se souvenir **de lui**.*
Did you know him? It is easy to remember him.

⚠ **En** can also be an adverb of place (= "from there") or a preposition (= "in"):

Êtes-vous allés chez elle? J' en *viens.*

adverb of place

Have you been to her place? I have just come from there.

Je vais en *ville.*

preposition

I'm going into town.

THE PERSONAL PRONOUN "Y"

The invariable personal pronoun **y** has the meaning of "to that person", "to that thing", "to that" (neuter). It usually refers to an idea or a thing and has the following functions:

– indirect object of a person: *L'avez-vous pris comme ami? Pour moi, je ne m'**y** fierais pas.*/Have you become friends with him? For myself, I wouldn't trust him.: "*y*" here is the indirect object of "*fierais*" (= I would not trust myself to him);

– indirect object of a thing: *Penses-tu à ce que je t'ai dit? J'**y** pense.*/Are you thinking about what I told you? I am thinking about it.: "*y*" is the indirect object of "*pense*" (I am thinking of that).

⚠ **Y** can also be an adverb of place (with the meaning of "there"):

*Connaissez-vous le Portugal? Je n'**y** suis pas allé.*
Do you know Portugal? I have not been there.

POSITION OF THE PERSONAL PRONOUN SUBJECT

● The personal pronoun subject is normally positioned before the verb. It can only be separated from the verb by a pronoun complement or the first part of a negation:

Je le **connais** de longue date.   **Je** n'y **suis** pas allé.
I have known him for a long time.   I didn't go there.

● The stressed personal pronoun subject can be placed after the verb:

>Je **saurai** lui répondre, **moi**./I could answer him. ("*moi*" is the subject of "*saurai*", like "*je*").

● The unstressed personal pronoun subject is placed after the verb or between the auxiliary and the participle in the compound tense in three cases:

– in interrogative or exclamative sentences:

>Que lui **avez-vous** dit?   **Puisse**-t-**elle** guérir vite!
>What did you say to him?   May she get well quickly!

– in interpolated clauses:

>Ce n'est pas ta faute, dis-**tu**./It's not your fault, you say. ("*dis-tu*" is an interpolated clause);

– in clauses beginning with **du moins, peut-être, au moins, en vain, aussi, à peine, ainsi**, etc.:

>**Peut-être** trouverez-**vous** un appui.
>Perhaps you will find some support.

>**À peine** avait-**il** terminé que je partis.
>Hardly had he finished that I left.

POSITION OF THE PERSONAL PRONOUN COMPLEMENT

● The unstressed personal pronoun complement is placed before the verb, except in the affirmative form of the imperative:

>Elle **le considéra** longuement.   Je ne **l'ai** pas **vu**.
>She looked at it a long time.   I haven't seen him.

>Ne **le prenez** pas.   but   **Prenez-le**.
>Don't take it.   Take it.

● The stressed personal pronoun complement is placed after the verb:

>Il me **plaît**, à **moi**, d'agir ainsi.
>For myself, it pleases me to act this way.

>**Envoyez-moi** le paquet par la poste.
>Send me the parcel by the post.

● When more than one pronoun are object complements of the same verb, the indirect object is placed nearest to the verb:

>Nous le **lui avons répété** cent fois./We have told him that a hundred times. ("*le*" is direct object, "*lui*" is indirect object).

In the imperative, the positioning is reversed:

>**Donnez**-le-**lui**./Give it to him.

Repetition of the Personal Pronoun

PERSONAL PRONOUN SUBJECT

The personal pronoun subject is usually repeated in front of each verb:

> **Elle** écouta en silence, puis **elle** réfléchit quelques instants.
> She listened in silence, and then she thought for a while.

This repetition is not obligatory when the verbs are placed next to each other or are coordinated by the conjunctions **et, ou, mais**:

> **Elle** agissait sans réflexion **et** s'étonnait de ses mésaventures.
> She acted without thinking and was surprised by her misfortunes.

⚠ There is no repetition when the verbs are linked by the conjunction **ni**:

> **Il** ne le saluait **ni** ne lui parlait jamais.
> He never greeted him nor spoke to him.

PERSONAL PRONOUN COMPLEMENT

The pronoun complement is usually respected before each verb:

> Elle **me** comprend et **m'**approuve.
> She understands me and approves of me.

There is always repetition when the two pronouns have a different function:

> Il **me** voit et **me** tend la main.
> He sees me and offers me his hand.

The personal pronoun complement is not repeated in the compound tenses of verbs when the auxiliary itself is not repeated, but with the condition that the pronoun complement has the same function:

> Elle **m'** a compris et **m'** a approuvé.
> direct object   direct object
> of "a compris"   of "a approuvé"

→ Elle **m'a** compris et approuvé: a single pronoun and a single auxiliary;

Il m'a vu et m'a tendu la main.: the "m'" direct object of "a vu" and the "m'" complement of "a tendu" have different functions, they are therefore repeated.

Reiteration of the Noun or the Pronoun by a Personal Pronoun

● The noun or the pronoun subject or complement can be highlighted by placing it at the beginning of the sentence. In this case, it is reiterated next to the verb by a pronoun subject or a pronoun complement:

> **Jeanne**, nous l'aimons beaucoup./Jeanne, we like her very much.

Toi, je **te** connais bien.   **Lui**, **il** est malin.
You, I know you well.   Him, he's smart.

● The noun subject can be placed after the verb in impersonal constructions:

> **Il** manque deux **cartes**./There are two cards missing. ("il" anticipates "cartes"; "il" is the apparent subject; "cartes" is the real subject of "manque").

THE EXPLETIVE PERSONAL PRONOUN

● The pronoun complement of the 1st or the 2nd person can be used without any real grammatical function in order to emphasize the speakers personal interest in the action or to draw his listener's attention:

> Regardez-**moi** ce spectacle!/Look at this show!

> On **vous** le fit tournoyer en l'air et maintes fois retomber sur le drap tendu.
> He was tossed in the air and made to fall many times into an open blanket.

● The personal pronoun appears without any real grammatical value, in a number of different expressions:

> Il s'**en** est pris à moi.   Bravo, vous **l**'emportez!
> He took it out on me.   Well done, you have won!

Relative Pronouns and Adjectives

The relative pronoun usually re-places a noun or pronoun placed before it. It is also a word which introduces a clause (see section "Structure of the sentence"). Its use is quite common, unlike the relative adjective which is used in only a few syntactic structures.

Role of relative pronouns

In a complex sentence, the relative pronoun replaces a noun or a pronoun called the "antecedent", expressed in the preceding clause. It sets up a relationship between this clause and the second one, called the "relative", which completes or explains the antecedent:

> *Il régnait un* silence *dont* chacun finissait par s'inquiéter.
>
> antecedent   pronoun
> relative

There prevailed a silence which eventually troubled everybody.

In this sentence, *"dont"*, the relative pronoun, replaces *"silence"*: every-body was troubled by this silence after a while. The relative clause which begins with *"dont"*, completes the noun *"silence"*, which is the antecedent of *"dont"*.

NOTE : The antecedent is sometimes not expressed (particularly in sayings and proverbs); in this case the relative pronoun has an indefinite meaning: *Qui dort, dîne.* (= *celui qui dort*)/A sleep is as good as a meal.
If it were expressed the subject of *"dîne"* would be *"celui"*, antecedent of *"qui"*.

Forms of relative pronouns

The relative pronoun, which has a simple form and a compound form, fol-lows the gender and number of its antecedent. This antecedent can be a noun (masculine and feminine) or a pronoun (masculine, feminine or neuter):

> *Les rose**s que** tu as cueillies sont belles.*/The roses you have picked are beautiful: *"que"*, the relative pronoun, is feminine plural, like *roses*, its antecedent, so that *"cueillies"* agrees.

> *As-tu vu l'importance de **ce** à **quoi** tu t'engages?*/Have you seen the importance of what you are undertaking? *"quoi"*, relative pro-noun, neuter singular like its antecedent, the neuter demonstrative pronoun *"ce"*.

NOTES :
1. The neuter gender has no compound form but one extra simple form (***quoi***).
2. ***Que*** elides to ***qu'*** in front of a vowel or a silent **-h**.

85

	Masculine	Feminine	Neuter
simple forms	qui	qui	qui
	que	que	que
			quoi
	dont	dont	dont
	où	où	où
compound forms	lequel, lesquels	laquelle, lesquelles	
	duquel, desquels	de laquelle, desquelles	
	auquel, auxquels	à laquelle, auxquelles	

USES OF RELATIVE PRONOUNS

The relative pronoun has all the functions of a noun in the relative clause it introduces.

▬▬ "QUI"

"*Qui*" can be masculine, feminine or neuter, singular or plural, and has the following functions in the relative clause:

– subject: *Je fais ce **qui** me plaît.*/I do what I like to do.: "*qui*", relative pronoun, neuter singular is the subject of "*plaît*";
– noun complement: *C'est un homme à la parole de **qui** on peut se fier.*/He's a man whose word can be trusted.; "*qui*", relative pronoun, masculine singular, is complement of the noun "*parole*";
– indirect object: *Connaissez-vous la personne de **qui** je parlais?*/Do you know the person I was talking about?; "*qui*", relative pronoun, masculine singular, is indirect object of "*parlais*";
– adverbial phrase: *Cet ami pour **qui** j'ai reporté mon voyage m'a fait faux bond.*/This friend for whom I put back my trip has let me down.; "*qui*", relative pronoun, masculine singular, is an adverbial phrase complementing "*ai reporté*".

⚠ "*Qui*" as a complement, can only have an antecedent which is the name of a person or a personified object.

▬▬ "QUE"

"*Que*" can be masculine, feminine or neuter, singular or plural, and has the following functions in the relative clause:

– predicate of subject: *La rusée **qu'**elle est a deviné.*/Clever woman that she is, she guessed.; "*que*", relative pronoun, feminine singular, is the predicate of "*elle*";

– direct object: *Elle saisit la main* **que** *je lui tendais.*/She seized the hand I offered her.; *"que"*, relative pronoun, feminine singular, is the direct object of *"tendais"*;

– adverbial time phrase: *Du temps* **que** *nous étions étudiants...*/At the time when we were students...; *"que"* relative pronoun, masculine singular, is an adverbial time phrase of *"étions"*.

■■■"QUOI"

"Quoi" is neuter singular (the antecedents are: **rien, ce, cela**) and can have the following functions in a relative clause:

– indirect object or adverbial phrase: *Voilà, précisément, ce à* **quoi** *je réfléchissais.*/That is exactly what I was thinking about.; *"quoi"*, relative pronoun, neuter singular, is the indirect object of *"réfléchissais"*;

– adjective complement: *Il n'est rien à* **quoi** *je ne sois prête.*/There is nothing for which I am not prepared.: *"quoi"*, relative pronoun, neuter singular, is the complement of the adjective *"prête"*.

NOTE : *"Quoi"* is used without an antecedent in different expressions: *"grâce à quoi"*/thanks to which, *"sans quoi"*/without which, *"moyennant quoi"*/ in return for which, *"c'est à quoi"*/it's to which.

■■■"DONT"

"Dont" is masculine, feminine or neuter, singular or plural and has the following functions in the relative clause:

– noun complement: *Elle raconta la scène* **dont** *elle avait été le témoin.*/She described the scene, which she had witnessed.: *"dont"*, relative pronoun, feminine singular, is complement of the noun *"témoin"*;

⚠ *"Dont"* cannot normally be the complement of a noun introduced by a preposition.

– adjective complement: *Je vous donne un travail* **dont** *vous me semblez capable.*/I am giving you some work, which you seem to me capable of.; *"dont"*, relative pronoun, masculine singular, is the complement of the adjective *"capable"*;

– agent: *Elle s'adressa aux amis* **dont** *elle était entourée.*/She spoke to the friends that she had around her.; *"dont"*, relative pronoun, masculine plural, is the agent of *"était entourée"*;

– adverbial phrase (cause): *C'est une maladie* **dont** *on ne meurt plus aujourd'hui.*/It's a disease one does not die from today.; *"dont"*, relative pronoun, feminine singular, is an adverbial phrase of cause of *"meurt"*;

– adverbial phrase (place/origin): *La famille* **dont** *je descends est originaire du Maine.*/The family I am descended from originally came from Maine.: *"dont"*, relative pronoun, feminine singular, is an adverbial phrase of means of *"descend"*;

– adverbial phrase (means and manner): *Il se saisit d'une pierre* **dont** *il le frappa.*/He seized a stone with which he hit him.: *"dont"*, relative pronoun, is an adverbial phrase of means of *"frappa"*;

– indirect object: *C'est une aventure* **dont** *elle se souvient fort bien.*/It is an adventure which she remembers well.; *"dont"*, relative pronoun, feminine singular, is an indirect object of *"se souvient"*.

■ "OÙ"

"Où" can only be used with things, it replaces the relative pronoun *"lequel"* preceded by a preposition and can have the following functions:

– adverbial phrase of place: *Le village où* (= in which) *il s'est retiré se trouve loin de l'autoroute.*/The village he withdrew to, is far from the highway:; *"où"*, relative pronoun, masculine singular, is an adverbial phrase of place of *"s'est retiré"*;

– adverbial phrase of time: *Il a fait froid la semaine où* (= during which) *vous êtes partis.*/It was cold the week (during which) you left.: *"où"*, relative pronoun, is an adverbial phrase of time of *"êtes partis"*.

NOTE : *"D'où"* is used without an antecedent, with the meaning of "from what", when drawing conclusions: *D'où je déduis que…*/ From which I deduce that…

■ "LEQUEL"

"Lequel" and the other compound forms (*auquel, duquel, laquelle, de laquelle, lesquels, desquels, auxquels, lesquelles, desquelles, auxquelles*) are used:

– when the antecedent is a noun and the relative is preceded by a preposition: *La **persévérance avec laquelle** elle a travaillé ne nous a pas étonnés.*/The perseverance with which she worked did not surprise us.;

– in place of *"que"* or *"qui"* when there is a possible ambiguity: *Je connaissais fort bien le fils de sa voisine, **lequel** avait les mêmes goûts.*/I knew very well his neighbour's son, who had the same interests.: *"qui avait les mêmes goûts"* would be ambiguous since *"qui"* could stand for *"fils"* or *"voisine"*;

– in place of *"dont"*, complement of a noun, itself a direct object: *Prenez soin de ces dossiers, **de la perte desquels** vous auriez à répondre.*/Take good care of these files, the loss of which you would be held responsible for.

P**LACE OF THE RELATIVE**

The relative pronoun, whether preceded or not by a preposition, is placed at the head of the relative clause and immediately after the antecedent:

> *Elle revoyait en rêve cette **maison dont** elle connaissait chaque pierre.*
> She would see again in her dreams this house every stone of which was known to her.

The relative pronoun is separated from its antecedent when the latter is followed by an adjective, by a noun complement or when it is the complement of a noun, which is itself an indirect object:

> *Je **la** vis **qui** ramassait un petit bout de ficelle.*
> I saw her who was picking up a little piece of string.

> *Il aimait la **musique**, à l'étude de **laquelle** il se consacrait.*
> He loved music, the study of which he devoted himself to.

In literature writers sometimes separate the antecedent from the relative (this is not possible in English):

> *Alors l'**arbre** s'écroula, **que** la foudre avait frappé.*
> Then the tree that the lightning had struck, fell down.

REPETITION OF THE RELATIVE PRONOUN

The relative pronoun is repeated when two or more relatives are coordinated or placed next to each other and when the function of the relative is not the same throughout or when the clauses are long:

> *Je vous conseille de lire ce **livre que** j'ai acheté la semaine dernière et **dont** j'aime beaucoup le sujet.*/I recommend you read this book which I bought last week and the subject of which I like very much.

The *"que"* here is the direct object of *"ai acheté"*; *"dont"* is the complement of the noun *"sujet"*.

NOTE : The relative pronoun is not repeated when the clauses are short and when it has the same function throughout:

> *Le **paysan** qui me servait de guide et ne me parlait guère me montra du doigt le village.*/The peasant who acted as my guide and who rarely spoke to me pointed out the village to me. (= *qui me servait de guide et qui ne me parlait guère*: *"qui"* is subject in each case).

INDEFINITE RELATIVES

The indefinite pronouns are: **quiconque, qui que, qui que ce soit qui, quoi que** (in two words); they are used without antecedent, with the meaning "every man who", "every thing that", etc.:

> ***Quiconque** cherchera, trouvera.*
> Whoever seeks, shall find.

> ***Quoi que** vous disiez, je m'en tiendrai à ma première idée.*
> Whatever you may say, I shall stick with my first idea.

> ***Qui que ce soit qui** vienne, dites que je suis occupé.*
> Whoever comes, tell them I'm busy.

NOTES :

1. *"Quiconque"* is sometimes used as an indefinite pronoun with the meaning "no matter who": *Défense à **quiconque** de pénétrer*/All entry forbidden (= whoever you are).

2. *"Quel que"* is an indefinite relative adjective, where *"quel"* is variable and agrees with the subject of the verb; it introduces a concessive clause in the subjunctive:

> ***Quelle que** soit votre **appréhension,** vous ne pouvez éviter cette rencontre.*
> However apprehensive you may feel, you cannot avoid this meeting.

*Quelles qu'aient été vos **erreurs** passées, je vous excuse.*
Whatever mistakes you may have made in the past, I forgive you.

Placed immediately in front of the verb *"être"*, **quel que** is written in two words.

RELATIVE ADJECTIVES

The relative adjective, which has the same form as the relative pronoun *"lequel"*, is rarely used and is restricted to legal language or to the expression *"auquel cas"*. It always agrees in gender and number with the word it refers to:

*Après avoir entendu les témoins, **lesquels témoins** ont déclaré...*
Having heard the witnesses, the said witnesses have stated...

*S'il pleuvait ce soir, **auquel cas** je ne pourrais pas venir...*
If it rains this evening, in which case I shall not be able to come...

INTERROGATIVE PRONOUNS AND ADJECTIVES

Interrogative pronouns invite the interlocutor to designate who or what the question applies to:
Qui as-tu rencontré?/ Who have you met? *De quoi parlez-vous?/* What are you talking about?
It could be a direct question; in which case the sentence finishes with a question mark:
À qui faut-il adresser cette réclamation?/ To whom should this complaint be made? (*"qui"*, interrogative pronoun in the direct form).

The question could be indirect; a sentence of this type depends on verbs like *"demander"* /to ask, *"savoir"*/to know, etc. and does not have a question mark:
Je demande à qui il faut adresser cette réclamation./
I am asking who this complaint should be sent to. (*"qui"* interrogative pronoun in the indirect form).
The interrogative adjective introduces an indication of the quality of the person who, or the thing which, the question addresses.

FORMS OF INTERROGATIVE PRONOUNS

The interrogative pronoun has normal and insistent forms. These forms vary with number (singular and plural) and with gender: masculine, feminine or neuter (designating imprecise things or ideas).

		Normal form			Insistent form	
		Masculine	Feminine	Neuter	People	Things
simple forms	sing.	*qui?*	*qui?*	*quoi? que?* *ce qui, ce que* (indirect question)	*qui est-ce qui? qui est-ce que? lequel est-ce qui?*	*qu'est-ce qui? qu'est-ce que? de quoi est-ce que?* (etc.)
	plur.	*qui?* (rare)	–			
compound forms	sing.	*lequel duquel auquel*	*laquelle de laquelle à laquelle*	–	–	–
	plur.	*lesquels desquels auxquels*	*lesquelles desquelles auxquelles*			

NOTES :
1. In spoken language the insistent form has become the usual form of direct question.
2. *Que* becomes *qu'* before a vowel or silent **h-**.

USES AND FUNCTIONS
OF INTERROGATIVE PRONOUNS

■ "QUI"

The pronoun "*qui*" concerns questions about a person and keeps this form in both direct and indirect questions (see "Interrogative clauses" p. 156); it can have the following functions:

	Direct questions	Indirect questions
subject	*Qui frappe à la porte?* Who's knocking at the door?	*Je demande qui frappe à la porte.* I'm asking **who's** knocking at the door.
complement	*Qui êtes-vous?* Who are you?	*Je demande qui vous êtes.* I'm asking **who** you are.
direct object	*Qui verra-t-on à la fête?* Who will we see at the party?	*Je demande qui l'on verra.* I'm asking **who** we're going to see.
indirect object 1	*À qui doit-on s'adresser?* Who should we speak to?	*Je demande à qui l'on doit s'adresser.* I'm asking **who** we should speak to.
noun complement	*De qui a-t-on pris l'avis?* From whom did you get advice?	*Je demande de qui l'on a pris l'avis.* I'm asking **who** we got advice from.
adjectival complement	*De qui est-il jaloux?* **Who** is he jealous of?	*Je demande de qui il est jaloux.* I'm asking **who** he is jealous of.
agent	*Par qui fut-elle nommée?* Who was she nominated by?	*Je demande par qui elle fut nommée.* I'm asking **who** nominated her.
indirect object 2	*À qui donne-t-on le prix?* Who is being given the prize?	*Je ne sais pas à qui on donne le prix.* I don't know **who** they are giving the prize to.
adverbial complement	*Avec qui vient-elle?* Who is she coming with?	*Je ne sais pas avec qui elle vient.* I don't know **who** she is coming with.

■ "QUE"

The pronoun "*que*" concerns questions about a person, a thing or an idea; it becomes **ce qui**, **ce que** in indirect questions and can have the following functions:

	Direct questions	Indirect questions
subject	*Que se passe-t-il?* What's happening?	*Je demande ce qui se passe.* I'm asking what's happening.
complement	*Qu'est-il devenu?* What became of him?	*Je me demande ce qu'il est devenu.* I am wondering what became of him.
direct object	*Que désirez-vous?* What do you want?	*Je demande ce que vous désirez.* I'm asking what you want.
adverbial complement	*Que coûte ce livre?* What's the price of this book?	*Je demande ce que coûte ce livre.* I'm asking what this book costs.

92

▰▰ "QUOI"

The pronoun *"quoi"* concerns questions about a thing or an idea; it becomes **ce que, quoi** in indirect questions and can have the following functions:

	Direct questions	Indirect questions
subject	*Quoi de nouveau?* What's new?	*Je demande ce qu'il y a de nouveau.* I'm asking whether there is anything new.
direct object	*Quoi répondre?* What's the answer?	*Je ne sais quoi répondre.* I don't know what to say.
indirect object 1	*À quoi cela peut-il servir?* What's the use of that?	*Je ne sais à quoi cela peut servir.* I don't know what it can be used for.
agent	*Par quoi est-elle émue?* What's moved her?	*Je ne sais par quoi elle est émue.* I don't know what has moved her.
indirect object 2	*À quoi doit-il son échec?* What's his setback due to?	*Je ne sais à quoi il doit son échec.* I don't know what caused his setback.
adverbial complement	*Sur quoi avez-vous parlé?* What did you speak about?	*Je ne sais sur quoi il a parlé.* I don't know what he spoke about.

▰▰ "LEQUEL"

The pronoun *"lequel"* asks for a designation of a person or a thing; it keeps the same form in both direct and indirect questions and can have the following functions:

	Direct questions	Indirect questions
subject	*Lequel d'entre vous désire me parler?* Which of you wants to speak to me?	*Je ne sais lequel d'entre vous désire me parler.* I don't know which of you wants to speak to me.
direct object	*Lequel de ces deux livres préfères-tu?* Which of these two books do you prefer?	*Je ne sais lequel de ces deux livres tu préfères.* I don't know which of these two books you prefer.
indirect object	*Auquel des deux songez-vous?* Which of the two are you thinking about?	*Je ne sais auquel des deux vous songez.* I don't know which of the two you're thinking about.
noun complement	*Duquel de ces fruits préférez-vous le parfum?* Of which of these fruits do you prefer the flavor?	*Je vous demande duquel de ces fruits vous préférez le parfum.* I'm asking you of which of these fruits you prefer the flavour.
adjectival complement	*Auquel de ces emplois paraît-elle le plus apte?* Which job does she seem more suited to?	*Je vous demande auquel de ces emplois elle paraît le plus apte.* I'm asking you which of these jobs she seems more suited to.

agent	Par *lequel* des deux avez-vous été accompagnée? Which of the two did you go with?	*Je ne sais par **lequel** des deux vous avez été accompagnée.* I don't know which of the two you went with.
indirect object	***Auquel** des deux avez-vous donné ce livre?* To which of the two did you give this book?	*Je ne sais **auquel** des deux vous avez donné ce livre.* I don't know which of the two you gave this book to.

Forms of interrogative and exclamative adjectives

The interrogative adjective has the form *quel* in the masculine and *quelle* in the feminine (plural: *quels* and *quelles*). It agrees in gender and number with the noun it relates to and preceeds.

> De *quelle province* êtes-vous originaire?/Which region do you come from?

"*Quel*" can either be attributive or predicative:

> *Quel jour viendrez-vous? Quel est cet arbre?*
> Which day are you coming? What kind of tree is that?

NOTE : The interrogative adjective can also be used as an exclamative adjective expressing admiration, surprise, indignation, etc.:

> *Quel beau fruit! Quelle fut sa surprise!*
> What a nice fruit! How surprised he was!

INDEFINITE PRONOUNS AND ADJECTIVES

| Indefinite pronouns indicate a being, thing or idea in a vague and indeterminate way. Indefinite adjectives precede a | noun to express an imprecise idea of quantity, quality, resemblance or difference. |

FORMS OF INDEFINITE PRONOUNS

Indefinite pronouns can be masculine, feminine or neuter:

> *Quelqu'un a sonné à la grille du jardin./*Someone's ringing at the garden gate.: *"quelqu'un"*, masculine;

> *Aucune d'entre elles n'osait intervenir./*Not one of them dared to intervene.: *"aucune"*, feminine;

> *Elle n'en a rien su./*She knew nothing about it.: "rien", neuter.

Masculine	Feminine	Neuter
aucun, nul, personne, n'importe qui, je ne sais qui, certains, plus d'un, plusieurs, l'un, l'autre, les uns, les autres, un autre, d'autres, autrui, on, quelqu'un, quelques-uns, chacun, tel, tels, le même, les mêmes, tout, tous, quiconque	aucune, nulle, personne, n'importe qui, je ne sais qui, l'une, l'autre, les unes, les autres, une autre, d'autres, on, quelqu'une, quelques-unes, chacune, telle, telles, la même, les mêmes, toute, toutes	rien n'importe quoi, je ne sais quoi, quelque chose, tout

FUNCTIONS OF INDEFINITE PRONOUNS

Indefinite pronouns can have nearly all the functions that nouns have:

– subject: *Nul ne l'avait vue./*Nobody had seen her.: *"nul"*, indefinite pronoun, masculine, is the subject of *"avait vue"*;

– direct object: *Il recevait n'importe qui./*He welcomed anybody.: *"n'importe qui"*, indefinite pronoun, masculine, direct object of *"recevait"*;

– indirect object: *Ne vous fiez pas à certains./*There are some you cannot trust.: *"certains"*, indefinite pronoun, masculine plural, indirect object of *"fiez"*;

– second object: *Donnez à chacun sa part./*Let everyone have his share.: *"chacun"*, indefinite pronoun, masculine singular, second object of *"donnez"*;

– agent: *Je ne suis connue de **personne** ici.*/Nobody knows me here.: *"personne"*, indefinite pronoun, masculine singular, agent of *"suis connue"*;

– adverbial complement: *Elle vient avec **quelqu'un**.*/She's coming with someone.: *"quelqu'un"*, indefinite pronoun, masculine singular, adverbial complement supporting *"vient"*.

FORMS OF INDEFINITE ADJECTIVES

The indefinite adjective is related to the noun it supports and agrees with it both in gender and number:

> *Elle n'a jamais eu **aucun** ami.*/She's never had a friend.: *"aucun"*, masculine singular, related to *"ami"*;

> *En **certaines** circonstances, il faut être prudent.* / In some instances, you have to be careful.: *"certaines"*, feminine plural, related to *"circonstances"*.

It can have the following forms, in relation to the idea it expresses:

Expression	Masculine	Feminine
quality	certain(s), n'importe quel(s), je ne sais quel(s), quelque, quelconque	certaine(s), n'importe quelle(s), je ne sais quelle(s), quelque, quelconque
quantity	aucun, pas un, nul, divers, différents, certains, plusieurs, plus d'un, maint(s), quelques, chaque, tout, tous	aucune, pas une, nulle, diverses, différentes, certaines, plusieurs, plus d'une, mainte(s), quelques, chaque, toute, toutes
difference	autre	autre
resemblance	même(s), tel(s)	même(s), telle(s)

USE OF INDEFINITE PRONOUNS AND ADJECTIVES

In a general sense each word classed as indefinite falls into several different grammatical classes.

● ***Aucun, aucune***, indefinite pronoun or adjective, is always associated with the negative ***ne*** or the preposition ***sans***:

> *Il **n'**en est **aucun** qui sache mieux son rôle.* (pronoun)/Nobody knows his part better.

> ***Aucune démarche n'**a été faite.* (adjective)/Nothing has been done.

> *Elle a réussi **sans aucun effort**.* (adjective)/She succeeded without any effort.

NOTES:

1. "*Aucun*" used to mean "*quelque*", "*quelqu'un*" and was used without a negative; it is still used without a negative in skeptical phrases requiring the subjunctive, or in interrogatives or comparative systems:

*Elle doutait qu'**aucun** d'entre vous **réussît**.*
She had her doubts whether any of you would succeed.

*Connaissez-vous **aucun autre** moyen?*/Do you know any other way?

*Elle est plus qualifiée qu'**aucune autre** personne.*
She's more qualified than anyone else.

"*Aucun*" and "*nul*" can be used in the plural: *aucuns frais; nuls soucis.*
In literary language, the pronoun "***d'aucuns***" means "*certains*":

***D'aucuns** sont d'un avis différent du vôtre.*
Some have a point of view to you different from yours.

2. If it is necessary to use the negative form then the indefinite pronouns and adjectives ***pas un, pas une, nul, nulle***, should be used, and they should always be followed by the negative ***ne***:

***Pas un** assistant **ne** se leva pour le contredire. **Nul ne** le revit.*
Not one assistant got up to contradict him. No one saw him again.

When it means "having no value", ***nul*** is used as a qualifying adjective:

*Cette explication est **nulle**./*This explanation is useless.

● ***Autre, autrui.*** "*Autre*", indefinite pronoun or adjective, serves to make the distinction between a new person or thing, and the first person or thing considered:

*Une **autre** vous remplacera.* (pronoun)
You will be replaced by someone else.

*Venez au début de l'**autre semaine**.* (adjective)
Come at the beginning of the other week.

When it means "being different", ***autre*** is used as a qualifying adjective:
*Le résultat fut tout **autre**./*The result was completely different.
"*Autrui*", an indefinite pronoun only used as a complement in sententious phrases aimed at everyone else except oneself: *Ne fais pas à **autrui** ce que tu ne voudrais pas qu'on te fît./*Don't do to anyone else what you wouldn't do to yourself.

● ***Certain, certaine***, indefinite adjectives, and ***certains, certaines***, indefinite pronouns, have an indeterminate meaning:

***Certaine affaire** m'appelle à l'étranger.* (adjective)
Some business is taking me abroad.

***Certains** me l'on dit.* (pronoun)/Some (people) told me that.

When "*certain*" follows a noun it relates to, it is no longer an indefinite adjective, but a qualifying adjective meaning "assured", "non-dubious":

*Une **certaine réussite** reste toute relative.* (indefinite adjective)
Some success remains somewhat relative.

*Une **réussite certaine** ne l'est pas.* (qualifying adjective)
Sure success is not relative.

● **Chaque, chacun**. *"Chaque"*, an indefinite adjective, *"chacun"*, *"chacune"*, indefinite pronouns apply to everyone or everything in a group, but considered separately:

Chaque *phrase était ponctuée d'un geste.* (adjective)
Every sentence was punctuated with a gesture.

Chacune *de ces discussions éveillait en lui des souvenirs.* (pronoun)
Each of these discussions awoke old memories for him.

● **Divers, plusieurs**. *"Divers"* (or *"différents"*), *"maints"*, indefinite adjectives, *"plusieurs"* (or *"plus d'un"*), indefinite adjective or pronoun, indicate a large or small quantity, but are always expressed in the plural:

Divers *amis m'ont prévenu **maintes** fois.* (adjective)
Different friends have warned me several times.

Plusieurs *m'ont assuré de leur sympathie.* (pronoun)
Several people have assured me of their sympathy.

● **L'un, l'autre**, indefinite pronouns, indicating whoever or whatever is in isolation from the group:

L'un *lève la tête, **l'autre** griffone sur une page.*
One is looking up, the other is scribbling on a page.

"Ni l'un ni l'autre" means *"aucun des deux"*; *"l'un et l'autre"*, means *"tous les deux"*; *"l'un ou l'autre"*, means *"un des deux"*. *"L'un l'autre"* expresses reciprocity:

*Ils se haïssent **l'un l'autre**.*/They hate each other.

● **Même** is an indefinite adjective when it means:

– "similar to", or "identical" (in this case it is placed between the article and noun): *Elles prirent la **même** route.*/They took the same route.;
– "personally" (here it is linked by a hyphen to a personal pronoun which precedes it for emphasis): *Nous-**mêmes** nous avons ri.*/Even we laughed.;
– "precision" (here it comes, without a hyphen, after the noun or pronoun): *Il est venu le matin **même**.*/He came that very morning.;
– "to emphasize a point" (here it also comes, without a hyphen, after the noun or pronoun): *Elle est la prudence **même**.*/She is prudence itself.

⚠ *"Même"* is an adverb, and hence invariable, when it means:

– "also" (usually in front of the article and its associated noun, very rarely after): **Même** *les garçons peinaient.*/The boys were also struggling.;
– "even though" (in front of an adjective): **Mêmes** *ruinés, ils avaient leur fierté.*/Even though ruined, they had their pride.;
– "in addition, moreover" (in front of the verb): *Elle le vit et **même** lui parla.*/She saw him and, moreover, spoke to him.

NOTE : "*Même*", if preceded by the definite article, can be an indefinite pronoun: *Ce n'est pas le même que le tien.* / It's not the same as yours.

● *On*, an indefinite pronoun is always used in the subject form, referring to one person or several people in an imprecise way:

> *On entendait courir dans la rue.*
> You could hear running in the street.

In spoken or written language, with an actual value attached (modesty, sympathy, irony, etc.), the pronoun "*on*" can replace the personal pronouns such as "*il*", "*elle*", "*nous*", "*vous*", "*ils*", "*elles*", "*je*", "*tu*". In this case, the adjective (or the predicative participle), where appropriate, agrees with the feminine or plural aspect built into "*on*", but the verb (or the auxiliary) remains singular:

> *On est bien spirituelle aujourd'hui!* (here "*on*" represents a woman)./She is very witty today.

> *On a été retardés par l'orage.* (here "*on*" = we: informal use)
> We were held up by the storm.

NOTES :

1. Sometimes the form "*l'on*" is used, especially in formal language, and in particular after *et, ou, où, qui, que, quoi, si*: *Qu'on s'adresse à qui l'on voudra*/Go and ask whoever you want…; *Si l'on n'y prend garde…* / If we do not take care about it…
2. The pronoun *on* is often treated as a personal pronoun in the subject form.

● *Personne, rien*, indefinite pronouns, are always accompanied by the negative "*ne*" or preceded by the preposition "*sans*", with the meaning "nobody" or "nothing":

> *Personne ne l'avait entendue. Il n'a rien vu qui retînt son attention.*
> Nobody had heard her. He saw nothing to attract his attention.

> *Elle est revenue du magasin sans avoir rien acheté.*
> She came back from the shops having bought nothing.

NOTE : "*Personne*" and "*rien*" sometimes mean "*quelqu'un*" or "*quelque chose*" in an interrogative or conditional clause, etc., which comes from seventeenth century use: *Avez-vous rien entendu de plus plaisant?* / Have you ever heard anything more pleasant?

⚠ "*Personne*" and "*rien*" can be nouns when they are preceded by an article:

> *Une personne est venue me voir. Un rien l'amuse.*
> A person came to see me. The slightest thing amuses him.

● *Quelconque, quiconque.* "*Quelconque*", an indefinite adjective, "*quiconque*" an indefinite pronoun (which can also be an indefinite relative), mean "no matter what", "no matter who":

> *Ouvrez ce livre à une page quelconque.*
> Open this book at any page.

Il est à la portée de **quiconque** *de résoudre ce problème.*
It is within the reach of anyone to resolve this problem.

NOTE : If the idea of indetermination is emphasized, then *"n'importe qui"*, *"n'importe quoi"* is used: *Elle ferait* **n'importe quoi** *pour l'aider./* She would do anything to help him.

● **Quelque** is an indefinite adjective when it precedes a noun and means "several", "a certain quantity", "a certain number", "some":

Quelques *indiscrets lui auront raconté mon aventure.*
Some indiscreet people will have told him about my adventure.

When it precedes a noun and is followed by the relative *"que"*, it introduces a concessionary clause in the subjunctive:

Quelques *raisons que vous* **avanciez**, *vous ne me convaincrez pas.*
Whatever reasons you may put forward they will not convince me at all.

⚠ *"Quelque"* is an adverb, and hence invariable, when it means:
– "about": *Il y a* **quelque** *quarante ans./* He's about forty years old.;
– "much": **Quelque** *grands* **que** *soient ses efforts, elle ne saurait réussir./* However great her efforts, she will never make it.

● **Quelqu'un, quelqu'une, quelques-uns, quelques-unes**, indefinite pronouns, referring in the singular to an indeterminate person; in the plural they point to an indeterminate number:

Quelqu'un *aurait-t-il fait obstacle à ton projet?*
Has somebody hindered your plan?

Quelques-uns *l'avaient connue jadis.*
Some poeple had known her in the past.

● **Tel** is an indefinite adjective when it means "a certain...":

Telle *page était griffonnée,* **telle** *autre tachée d'encre.*
A certain page was scribbled on, another stained with ink.

NOTE : *"Tel"* is a qualifying adjective when it means:
– "similar", "the same as the preceding point": *Le jardin est* **tel** *que je l'avais imaginé./* The garden is just as I imagined it.: the conjunctive clause introduced by *"que"* is a comparative subordinate clause;
– "so important that...": *Ses paroles avaient une* **telle** *sincérité que tous furent émus./* His words were so sincere that everyone was moved.: the conjunction clause introduced by *"quoi"* is a consecutive clause.

"Tel" is an indefinite pronoun when it means "someone" (usually as an antecedent relative clause):

Tel *est pris qui croyait prendre./* The tables are turned.

NOTE : "*Tel*" is a demonstrative adjective or pronoun when it means "this", "that", "this one":

Tels furent les résultats de ses efforts./Such were the results of his efforts.

● ***Tout*** is an indefinite adjective when it means:

– "any" or "each", in the sense of "no matter what":

*À **tout** instant, je peux m'arrêter.*/At any moment, I can stop.

– "without exception":

Tous les élèves sont tenus de remettre des devoirs.

All pupils are obliged to hand in their homework.

NOTE :

1. "*Tout*" is a qualifying adjective when it means:
– "the whole" (situated before a noun and accompanied by a determiner): ***Toute** la famille est réunie.*/The whole family is reunited.
– "sole" (or "only") (no determiner in front of the following noun): *Pour **toute** excuse, elle allégua son ignorance.*/For her sole excuse, she pleaded ignorance.

2. "*Tout*" can also be a noun when, preceded by an article, it means: "the totality", "the whole": *Donnez-moi **le tout**.*/Give me it all.

"*Tout*" is an indefinite pronoun when it means:

– "everybody", "everything": ***Tous** sortiront de la salle.*/Everybody will leave the room.
– "no matter who", "no matter what": ***Tout** peut arriver.*/Anything can happen.

⚠ "*Tout*" is an adverb when it means: "very". Here it modifies an adjective, an adverb, a verb, or a noun:

*Des livres **tout** neufs. Il marchait **tout** doucement.*
Brand new books. He walked very slowly.

As an adverb, "*tout*" remains invariable, except in front of feminine adjectives beginning with a consonant or an aspirated "**h-**":

*Elle s'arrêta **tout** étonnée, **toute** honteuse. Des fleurs **toutes** blanches.*
She stopped very astonished, very ashamed. Completely white flowers.

However, in everyday language, agreement is accepted before adjectives starting with a vowel or a mute "**h**": *la province **tout** entière* or *toute entière*/the whole region.

VERBS

The verb is a word with an inflectional form which expresses an action either enacted by the subject (*Je marchais seul dans la rue obscure.* / I was walking down alone the gloomy street.) or bearing on the subject (*Les pièces défectueuses seront remplacées.* / The faulty parts will be replaced.) or which shows the state of the subject (*Le ciel est nuageux.* / The sky is cloudy.). Such are the essential constituents of the verb group.

GENERAL TYPES OF VERB

There are two major types of verb:

● **action verbs** (the word "action" having a broad meaning):

> *Il le **reçut** avec politesse. La malade **a subi** une opération.*
> He received him politely. The patient underwent an operation.

● **stative verbs** which introduce in particular a complement to the subject:

> *Il **paraissait** désespéré. Elle **devenait** plus habile.*
> He seemed desperate. She became more skilful.

NOTE : The same verb can be expressed in either the active or stative form:
*Elle **éclaire** la pièce.* / She is lighting up the room.
*La pièce **est éclairée**.* / The room is lit.

● Other types of verb can also be recognized according to their meaning:

– verbs of opinion: *penser*/to think, *croire*/to believe, *juger*/to judge, etc.;
– verbs of utterance: *dire*/to say, *affirmer*/to affirm, etc;
– verbs of movement: *marcher*/to walk, *courir*/to run, *aller*/to go, etc.;
– verbs of exchange: *vendre*/to sell, *acheter*/to buy, etc.;
– verbs of change: *changer*/to change, etc.;
– verbs of perception: *voir*/to see, *entendre*/to hear, *sentir*/to feel, etc.

● **A verb phrase** is a group of words (verb + noun, infinite or adverb) which takes the place of a simple verb: *avoir envie, avoir l'air, faire peur, rendre service, tourner court, faire croire, il y a, il y avait*, etc.:

> *J'**ai envie** de ce livre.* / I want this book.

A group of words forms a verbal phrase when the noun involved is not preceded by an article or when it is impossible to insert a complement between the verb and the noun: *avoir l'air*/to look like, *faire peur*/to inspire fear, *mettre en cause*/to call into question (or to implicate).

TRANSITIVE AND INTRANSITIVE VERBS

A verb can be transitive or intransitive depending on the fact that it requires or not such or such kind of complement.

▬ TRANSITIVE VERBS

A verb is transitive when the associated action is related to a person or a thing, thus forming a direct object:

J'ouvre la porte.	Je sais que tu m'attends.
Direct object of *"ouvre"*	Direct object of *"sais"*
I open the door.	I know you are waiting for me.

● The object can directly follow the verb without the need of a preposition. It is then a direct object and the verb is a direct transitive one:

Elle **reprit** son **livre**. / She resumed her book.: *"livre"* is the direct object of *"reprit"*; *"reprit"* is a direct transitive verb.

● By using a preposition, the object can depend on the verb; then it becomes an indirect object; the verb is an indirect transitive:

Elle **pardonne à son fils**./ She has forgiven her son.: *"fils"* is the indirect object of *"pardonne"*; in this instance, *"pardonne"* is an indirect transitive verb.

⚠ A verb can sometimes be a direct transitive, sometimes an indirect transitive; the two constructions generally having a different meaning:

Il **manque** son but. (direct transitive)/He is missing his objective.

Il **manque** à sa parole. (indirect transitive)/He doesn't keep his word.

▬ INTRANSITIVE VERBS

A verb is intransitive when the action is not associated with an object, but remains limited to the subject:

Paule **part** pour la campagne. (*"partir"* is an intransitive verb)

Adverbial complement of place

Paule is leaving for the country.

Stative verbs are always intransitive:

Il **semblait** désolé./He seemed sorry.: *"sembler"* is intransitive; *"désolé"* is a predicative adjective of the subject *"il"*.

⚠ Intransitive verbs can be used in a transitive form:

Elle est déjà descendue. (*"descendre"*: intransitive form)
She's already down.

Elle a descendu les bagages. (*"descendre"*: transitive form)
She's brought the luggage down.

VOICE

A verb can be in active, passive or reflexive voice (or form). The only verbs which can appear in all three voices or forms are the active verbs which are direct and transitive. The stative and intransitive verbs only exist in the active voice; indirect transitive verbs are not generally passive: *j'écoute* / I listen (active voice); *je suis écouté* / I am listened to (passive voice); *je m'écoute* / I listen to myself (reflexive voice).

ACTIVE VOICE

A verb is in active voice when the subject represents a person or a thing doing the action:

L'enfant **court** dans la rue. / The child is running in the street.

or when the state of the subject is indicated by the verb:

Elle **restait** silencieuse. Paul **était devenu** pâle.
She remained silent. Paul had become pale.

PASSIVE VOICE

A verb is in the passive voice when the subject represents a person or thing subjected to the action indicated by the verb: here the verb is accompanied by the auxiliary "*être*":

Son fils **a été blessé** dans un accident.
Her son has been hurt in an accident.

In the passive voice the subject is the complementary object of the corresponding active expression (*Une pierre a blessé son fils.* / A stone has hurt his son.). The action is done by the agent (= the subject of the corresponding active expression), introduced by the prepositions **par** or **de**:

Le cri a été entendu **par tous les assistants**. / The cry has been heard by all those present.: "assistants" is the agent of "a été entendu".

But this complement cannot always be used:

Elle **a été punie** hier. / Yesterday she has been punished.: "a été punie" is not followed by an agent.

REFLEXIVE VOICE

A verb is in the reflexive voice when the subject is associated with a reflexive personal pronoun in the same person as the subject and placed before the verb:

Luc **se** regardait dans la glace. / Luc looked at himself in the mirror.

Relexive verbs are split into different categories according to their meaning.

104

PRONOMINAL VERBS MAINLY REFLEXIVE

These are verbs which only exist in the reflexive form or where the reflexive pronoun serves no grammatical function in the expression:

César ne put s'emparer de Gergovie./Caesar could not take over Gergovia.: *"s'emparer"* is only found in the reflexive form.

Il ne s'est pas aperçu de son erreur./He did not become aware of his mistake.: dans *"s'apercevoir"*, the pronoun serves no grammatical function. *"Apercevoir"* exists in the active form and has a different meaning to *"s'apercevoir"*.

TRUE REFLEXIVE VERBS

The subject performs an action related to oneself. The reflexive pronoun can be either a direct, indirect or second object:

Il se peigne./He's combing his hair.: *"se"*, direct object of *"peigne"*.

Elle s'accorde du repos./She is giving herself a rest.: *"se"*, second object or attributive complement of *"accorde"*.

NOTE : When a reflexive verb is used in the infinitive after *faire* or *laisser,* the reflexive pronoun is often omitted:

*Faites asseoir le client dans ce bureau. /*Invite the client to sit in this office. (= *Faites en sorte que le client s'assoie.*)

REFLEXIVE VERBS WITH A RECIPROCAL MEANING

Several people (or animate things) create an action between each other which is indicated by the verb. The reciprocal pronoun can be a direct, indirect or second object:

*Jeanne et Pierre ne se sont jamais vus. /*Jeanne and Peter have never seen each other: *"se"*, direct object of *"sont vus"*.

Ils ne se sont jamais nui l'un à l'autre./They've never harmed each other.: *"se"*, indirect object of *"sont nui"*.

REFLEXIVE VERBS WITH A PASSIVE VOICE

Some verbs can be used in the reflexive voice with a passive meaning:

Les fruits se vendent cher. (reflexive voice) = *Les fruits sont vendus cher.* (passive voice)/Fruit is expensive.

MOOD, TENSES, ASPECTS AND PERSON

The action or state expressed by the verb can be presented according to several characteristics: these being mood, tense or aspect. The action or state thus expressed is in relation to a person. People are either the participants in the communication (*je, tu, nous, vous*), or the object of the communication (*il, elle, ils, elles*).

MOOD AND TENSES

● The action can be presented in the present, past or future; this is the concept of tenses:

je lis (present); *j'ai lu* (past); *je lirai* (future) (*lire* = to read).

Simple tenses are the ones which are expressed in a unique verbal form:

Il lira; il lirait; je cours; nous allions (*aller* = to go).

Compound tenses are those which are expressed in a verbal form using an auxiliary and a past participle:

*Il **avait lu*** (active). *Ce livre **est connu de tous*** (passive).
He had read. Everybody knows this book.

Double compound tenses are formed by two auxiliaries and a past participle:

*Dès que **j'ai eu fini** mon devoir, je suis allé jouer.*
As soon as I had finished my homework, I went to play.

● The action can be presented as real, possible, required, desired; this is the concept of mood:

elle lit (real action): indicative; *lis* (action required): imperative;

elle lirait (possible action): conditional;

je demande qu'elle lise (action desired): subjunctive.

The "*personal mood*" is represented by the indicative, conditional, subjunctive, imperative, because the verbal form varies with the person.

The "*impersonal mood*" is represented by the participle and infinitive, because the verbal form does not vary with the person.

NOTE: Verbs for which some moods or tenses are lacking are called "defective verbs". Thus the verb "*déchoir*" is defective: it has no imperfect or imperative indicative.

Mood	Simple tenses		Compound tenses	
indicative	present	*je lis*	present perfect	*j'ai lu*
	imperfect	*je lisais*	pluperfect	*j'avais lu*
	past historic	*je lus*	past anterior	*j'eus lu*
	future	*je lirai*	future perfect	*j'aurai lu*
conditional	present	*je lirais*	past (1)	*j'aurais lu*
			past (2)	*j'eusse lu*
subjunctive	present	*que je lise*	past	*que j'aie lu*
	imperfect	*que je lusse*	pluperfect	*que j'eusse lu*
imperative	present	*lis; lisez*	past	*aie lu; ayez lu*
participle	present	*lisant*	past	*ayant lu*
infinitive	present	*lire*	past	*avoir lu*

ASPECTS

The action can be presented in two ways:

– as being in the course of doing something; this is the unfinished aspect:

> *On entend ce matin le bruit de la route.*
> This morning we can hear the noise of the highway.

– as already having been done at the moment it is expressed: this is the finished aspect:

> *On a réparé l'aspirateur./*The hoover has been repaired.

In the first example, *"entend"* is both in the present and unfinished (= *le bruit de la route s'entend*); in the second example, *"a réparé"* has present consequences and is finished (= *l'aspirateur se trouve actuellement réparé*).

Therefore the aspect goes with the tense; there is the unfinished past (like the imperfect in some of its uses), the finished past (like the past historic) and the unfinished present (very often the present perfect):

> *La tempête durait depuis huit jours.* (unfinished past)
> The storm had been going on for a week.

> *La tempête dura huit jours.* (finished past)
> The storm lasted a week.

> *La tempête s'est levée aujourd'hui.* (unfinished present)
> The storm got up today.

107

PERSON AND NUMBER

The verb form varies with its subject:

	Singular	Plural
1ˢᵗ person 2ⁿᵈ person 3ʳᵈ person	*je lirai* *tu liras* *il/elle lira*	*nous lirons* *vous lirez* *ils/elles liront*

⚠️ The imperative is the one personal mood which only comprises the 2ⁿᵈ person singular and plural and the 1ˢᵗ person plural.

IMPERSONAL VERBS

Verbs which are only in the 3ʳᵈ person singular, with the exception of those verbs referring to a being or a given object, are called impersonal verbs:

Il faut... Il pleut. Il neige. Ça sent bon, ici!

I, you, we, or they have to... It rains. It snows. It smells good here!

The impersonal verb is always used with the subject pronoun "*il*" or, informally, with the pronoun "*ça*".
Impersonal verbs can be a part of verbal phrases:

Il fait beau./It's nice weather.

NOTE : A verb can be said to be impersonal when it is used in the same conditions as an impersonal verb, while being personal, on an other hand, with an other meaning: *Il **arrive** souvent qu'un accident se produise à ce carrefour.*/ There's often an accident at this crossroads.: "*arrive*", being taken impersonally and meaning "it happens".

RADICAL AND ENDINGS

Simple verb forms are made up of a radical, which represents the idea contained in the verb, and an ending, which indicates the mood, tense and person. Dans *nous chantons,* **chant-** is the radical (found also in "***chanteur***", "***chantonner***") and **-ons** is the ending, indicating the present indicative and the 1ˢᵗ person plural (*chanter* = to sing).

● The ending is essentially variable; changing according to the person, tense or mood: *je chante; vous chant**erez**; ils chant**èrent**.*

● The radical is found by removing the ending of the infinitive:

chant -*er,* **fin** -*ir*/to finish, **entend** -*re*/to hear.

It is generally identical for all conjugations of a verb. But the radical can vary according to the mood or tense, and inside the same tense:

aller/to go: *je **vais**, nous **allons**, j'**irai**, que j'**aille**.*

Auxiliaries and Semi-auxiliaries

The auxiliary is a verb form which has lost its own significance and serves to express certain moods and tenses in another verb.
A distinction is made between the auxiliaries as such (*avoir et*

être): *J'ai lu.*/I have read. *Nous sommes arrivés.*/We have arrived.; and the auxiliaries of tense, aspect or mood, or semi-auxiliaries: *Je viens de lire.*/I have just read.

The auxiliaries "avoir" and "être"

The auxiliary *avoir* is used to form the compound tense of transitive verbs and most of the intransitive verbs in the active voice:

> *Nous avons entendu des cris. Elle a vécu deux ans à Toronto.*
> We heard cries. She's lived in Toronto for two years.

The auxiliary *être* is used to form the simple and compound tenses of verbs in the passive voice, the compound tenses of reflexive verbs and some intransitive verbs (*naître*/to be born, *mourir*/to die, *devenir*/to become, *aller*/to go, *partir*/to leave, etc.):

> *Il est surpris de ton arrivée. Le chien s'est jeté sur lui en aboyant.*
> Your arrival surprised him. The dog jumped on him barking as it did so.

> *Le loup est tombé dans le piège.*/The wolf fell into the trap.

NOTE : Some verbs are used as transitives with the auxiliary *"avoir"* and as intransitives with the auxiliary *"être"*.

> *Elle a monté les bagages.* (transitive)/She took the luggage up.
> direct object

> *Elle est montée au 3ᵉ étage.* (intransitive)/She went up to the 3rd floor.
> Adverbial phrase of place

Auxiliaries of mood or tense

Some verbs are used as auxiliaries to express a particular value for mood, aspect or tense. They are called "semi-auxiliaries".

● **Auxiliaries of mood:**

> *aller* = an order: *Vous allez me refaire cela.*/You are going to redo that for me.

> *devoir* = probability: *Le locataire doit être sorti.*/The tenant must have gone out.

> *pouvoir* = wish: *Puissiez-vous venir!*/May you come!

- **Auxiliaries of aspect or tense:**

  venir de = very recent past: *Elle **vient** de partir.*/She's just left.

  être en train de = action being done oneself: *Je **suis en train de** lire.*/I'm reading.

  être sur le point de = very near future: *J'étais **sur le point de** sortir.*/I was on the point of leaving.

  aller = near future: *Je **vais** lui parler.*/I'm going to speak to him.

CONJUGATIONS

Conjugating a verb means to make its form vary in relation to mood, tense or person. The verbs are classed according to the endings of tense and mood, and the variation in the root. With this classification the verbs can be regrouped according to the type of conjugation.

TYPES OF CONJUGATION

Three groups of verbs can be recognised in conjugation, according to the verbal form which presents the verbs in different moods and tenses:

1st group: **aimer**/to love =   verbs with the infinitive ending in **-er**

2nd group: **finir**/to finish =   -   -   -   -   -   **-ir**
(pres. part.-**issant**)

3rd group: **offrir**/to offer =   -   -   -   -   -   **-ir**
(pres. part.-**ant**)

recevoir/to receive =   -   -   -   -   -   **-oir**
prendre/to take =   -   -   -   -   -   **-re**

NOTE : The 1st and 2nd groups are rich in new verbs; contrary to the 3rd group which tends to be impoverished: from *téléphone* comes **téléphoner**; from *rouge*, **rougir**; but *se rappeler* (1st group) competes with *se souvenir* (3rd group): *Je me souviens de mon enfance; je me rappelle mon enfance./* I remember my childhood.

VERBAL FORMS IN NEGATIVE PHRASES

● In the simple verbal forms, the verb comes between the two parts of the negative *"ne... pas"*, *"ne... point"*, *"ne... que"*, *"ne... jamais"*, etc.:

> *Je **ne** comprends **pas** votre obstination.*
> I don't understand your obstinacy.

● In the compound verb forms, only the auxiliary comes in between:

> *Je **n'ai point** attendu votre conseil pour agir.*
> I didn't wait for your advice before acting.

● In the infinitive, the negative is preceded by the simple form:

> *Il sait **ne pas** insister quand il a tort.*
> He knows not to insist when he is wrong.

● The infinitive of ***avoir*** and ***être*** can be flanked by ***ne... pas***:

> *Il prétend **n'avoir pas** le temps* (or ***ne pas** avoir le temps*).
> He claims he doesn't have the time.

*Je regrette de **n'être pas** venu (or de **ne pas** être venu).*
I regret not having come.

VERB FORMS FOR INTERROGATIVE PHRASES

In direct interrogative clauses, the positioning of the pronoun after the verb can lead to modifications in spelling because of the pronunciation of some verb forms:

– change of the **-e** mute to **-é** (rarely used): *Je parle.* → *Parlé-je?*
– adding a **-t** to avoid the hiatus: *Acceptera-**t**-il?*

However, to avoid certain forms, the phrase ***est-ce-que...?*** is used in the 1st person, and often in others, to allow the subject to stay in front of the verb:

*****Est-ce-que** je pars tout de suite? **Est-ce-qu'**il acceptera?***
Do I leave at once? Will he accept?

NOTE : In phrases which are both interrogative and negative (interro-negative), the simple verbal form or the auxiliary come between the two elements of the negative:

*****Ne** viendra-t-elle **pas** demain? **Ne** l'avez-vous **pas** connu jadis?***
Isn't she coming tomorrow? Didn't you know him before?

SPECIAL FEATURES OF CONJUGATIONS

Verbs in the 1st group, all having the same ending as the model verb *"aimer"*/to love, sometimes give rise to special features, according to the form of the root. Verbs in the 2nd group conjugate around the model *"finir"*/to finish, with the sole exception of three verbs. Verbs in the 3rd group cannot be conjugated from a single model and have many special features.

1ST GROUP VERBS

■VERBS ENDING IN -CER, -GER

The verbs ending in **-cer** take a cedilla before **-a-** and **-o-**; verbs ending in **-ger** take an **-e-** after the **-g-** before **-a-** and **-o-**:

> *pla**c**er*/to place (present infinitive) – *je pla**ç**ais, nous placions* (imperfect indicative);

> *man**g**er*/to eat (present infinitive) – *je man**ge**ais, nous mangions* (imperfect indicative).

■VERBS ENDING IN -YER, -AYER

The verbs ending in **-yer** change the **-y-** into an **-i-** before a mute **-e-;** verbs ending in **-ayer** can keep the **-y-** before a mute **-e-:**

> *netto**y**er*/to clean (present infinitive) – *je netto**i**e, il/elle netto**i**e, nous nettoyons, ils netto**i**ent* (present indicative); *je netto**i**erai, nous netto**i**erons* (future indicative);

> *pa**y**er*/to pay (present infinitive) – *je pa**y**e (or pa**i**e), il/elle pa**y**e (or pa**i**e); nous payons, ils/elles pa**y**ent (pa**i**ent)* (present indicative); *je pa**y**erai (or pa**i**erai)* (future indicative).

■VERBS ENDING IN -ELER

The verbs ending in **-eler** double the **-l-** before a syllable containing a mute **-e-,** with the exception of: ***celer, ciseler, congeler, déceler, démanteler, écarteler, geler, marteler, modeler, peler,*** which change the mute **-e-** of the last but one syllable of the infinitive into an open **-è-:**

> *appeler*/to call (present infinitive) – *j'appe**ll**e, il/elle appe**ll**e, nous appelons, ils/elles appe**ll**ent* (present indicative);

> *peler*/to peel (present infinitive) – *je p**è**le, il/elle p**è**le, nous pelons, ils/elles p**è**lent* (present indicative).

VERBS ENDING IN -ETER

The verbs ending in **-eter** double the **-t-** before a syllable containing a mute **-e-,** with the exception of: ***acheter, corseter, crocheter, fureter, aleter, racheter,*** which change the **-e-** of the last but one syllable of the infinitive into an open **-è-**:

> *jeter/* to throw (present infinitive) – *je je**tte**, tu je**tte**s, il/elle je**tte**, nous jetons, ils/elles je**ttent*** (present indicative);

> *acheter/* to buy (present infinitive) – *j'ach**è**te, il/elle ach**è**te, nous achetons, ils/elles ach**è**tent,* (present indicative).

OTHER VERBS WHERE THE LAST BUT ONE SYLLABLE CONTAINS A MUTE -E- OR A CLOSED -É-

These verbs change the mute **-e-** or the closed **-é-** into an open **-è-** when the following syllable contains a mute **-e-,** except for the future and conditional form of verbs where the last but one syllable is a closed **-é-**:

> *semer/* to sow (present infinitive) – *je s**è**me, il/elle s**è**me, nous semons, ils/elles s**è**ment* (present indicative); *je s**è**merai, nous s**è**merons* (future indicative);

> *révéler/* (present infinitive) – *je rév**è**le, il/elle rév**è**le, nous révélons, ils/elles rév**è**lent* (present indicative); *je rév**é**lerai, nous rév**é**lerons* (future indicative).

THE IMPERATIVE

For verbs ending in **-er**, the second person singular of the imperative never takes an **-s**,

> except before **-en** and **-y**:

> *Parle**s-en**, va**s-y**.*/Speak of it, go.

2ND GROUP VERBS

Verbs of the 2nd group follow the model of the verb *"finir"*. There are only three verbs showing special features:

● ***haïr/***to hate keeps the diaerisis in all forms, except in the 1st, 2nd and 3rd person of the present indicative and the 2nd person singular of the imperative: *Je hais, tu hais, il/elle hait;*

● ***fleurir/***to flourish with the meaning of "prosper", forms its imperfect and present participle with the root **flor-**: *Les cités florissaient.* but *Les roses fleurissaient.;*

● ***bénir/***to bless which is regular, normally has the past participle, ***béni,*** except in the expressions *pain bénit, eau béni**te**.*

3RD GROUP VERBS

This group includes a small number of verbs, all irregular and in common use; there are no new verbs attached to any type of conjugation in this group.
Verbs in the 3rd conjugation show many irregularities, both in their roots and endings:

– modification of the root intervening during conjugation:

>*je **reçois**/*I receive, *nous **recevons**; je **meurs**/* I die, *nous **mourons**;*

– the simple past and the past participle present many different forms:

>*je con**duisis**/*I drove, *con**duit**; je **vis**/*I saw, ***vu**; je re**çus**/*I received, *re**çu**;*

>*je **fuis**/*I fled, ***fui**; je **fis**/* I made, ***fait**; je **pris**/*I took, ***pris**;*

– the present indicative and the imperative have various endings:

>***prendre**/*to take becomes *je **prends**, il/elle **prend*** (imperative: ***prends**);*

>***peindre**/*to paint becomes *je **peins**, il/elle **peint*** (imperative: ***peins**);*

>***savoir**/* to know becomes *je **sais**, il/elle **sait*** (imperative: *sache);*

– the only endings having the same form for all verbs are the imperfect and future indicative, present conditional and present participle:

>*je pren**ais**, je ven**ais**, il saura, elle offrira, elle pourrait, il voudrait*
>I took, I came, he will know, she will offer, she could, he would

– the imperfect subjunctive is always formed from the simple past:
je pris, que je prisse, j'aperçus, que j'aperçusse;

– the present and simple past of the indicative can lead to oral confusion in 1st, 2nd and 3rd person singular:

>*je **fuis**/*I flee or I fled, *tu **fuis**, il **fuit**; je **ris**/*I laugh or I laughed, *tu ris, elle **rit**.*

⚠ The imperative of verbs in the 3rd conjugation ending in a mute -**e**- takes an -**s** before -**en** and -**y**:

>*Cueille**s-en** quelques-unes./*Pick some of them.

THE INDICATIVE MOOD

The indicative mood is used to express an action or a state which are certain, real and general (*Il fait beau aujourd'hui.*/Today, the weather is fine.) or which are considered as such by the speaker or writer (*Il s'inquiète inutilement.*/ He gets worried needlessly).

THE PRESENT

The present expresses an action (or a state which exists) at the moment of speaking:

*Je **vois** de ma fenêtre la pluie qui **tombe** à verse.*
From my window, I can see it's pouring with rain.

PARTICULAR USES OF THE PRESENT

The present can also express:

– a general idea which is always true:

*Le sage **réfléchit** avant d'agir.*/The wise thinks before acting.

– an action which is habitually repeated:

*Le soir, je **lis** d'ordinaire jusqu'à minuit.*/In the evening, I usually read up to midnight.

– a past action which needs highlighting (dramatic or narrative present):

*Elle se promenait tranquillement sur la route; soudain **survient** une voiture.*
She was walking quietly along the road; suddenly a car appeared.

– an action which happens in the immediate future:

*Il **arrive** dans un instant.*/He's coming shortly.

– a future action after *si* introducing a conditional phrase where the main clause is in the future:

*Demain, s'il fait beau, nous **irons** voir le lever du soleil.*
Tomorrow, if it's nice, we will watch the sunrise.

THE FUTURE

The future expresses an action which is going to or about to happen, as opposed to the present (is happening) or the past (happened):

*Nous **verrons** bientôt revenir les beaux jours.*
The nice days will soon be back.

PARTICULAR USES OF THE FUTURE

The future can also be expressed as:

– a command (like the imperative):

> *Vous **prendrez** ces cachets tous les matins à jeun.*
> Take these pills every morning before eating.

– a present action, taking the sting out of a command (polite form):

> *Je vous **demanderai** de me laisser poursuivre mon exposé.*
> Would you please let me continue my talk.

– a past action following another past action (historic anticipation):

> *Montcalm fut vaincu à Quebec. De là **viendra** la perte de la Nouvelle-France.*
> Montcalm was beaten at Quebec. This was to lead to the loss of Nouvelle-France.

– a general idea, which is a permanent truth:

> *On ne **sera** jamais assez prudent.*/You can't be too careful.

– a future action following another future action:

> *Tu frapperas, et on t'**ouvrira**.*/Knock and someone will answer.

– a probable hypothesis, a supposition:

> *Qui a frappé? Ce **sera** la voisine.*/Who's knocking? It'll be the neighbour.

– an indignant protest:

> *Ils **auront** donc tous les droits!*/So, they'll have all the rights!

THE IMPERFECT

The imperfect indicates a past action considered over its duration:

> *Il **feuilletait** fébrilement son livre.*
> He leafed through the book feverishly.

PARTICULAR USES OF THE IMPERFECT

The imperfect can also indicate:

– a past action which repeats itself (repetition or habit):

> *La semaine il **rentrait**, **prenait** son journal et **se mettait** à lire sans dire un mot.*
> During the week, he would come home, pick up the newspaper, and start to read without saying a word.

– a past action which happens at the same time as another action expressed in the past historic (simultaneity):

> *Elle **dormait** encore profondément quand **sonnèrent** huit heures.*
> She was still sleeping deeply when eight o'clock rang.

- an action which happens suddenly in the past:

> *Il s'étendit sur son lit; cinq minutes après, le téléphone **sonnait**.*
> He stretched out on the bed; five minutes later, the telephone rang.

- in a past narrative, habitual aspects of a person or thing (descriptive):

> *Ses cheveux **tombaient** sur ses épaules.*
> His hair fell over his shoulders.

- in a conditional phrase introduced by *si*, the condition imposed or idea expressed by the main clause:

> *Elle n'accepterait pas **si** je lui **offrais** mon aide.*
> She wouldn't accept even if I offered my help.

- a regret:

> *Ah! s'il **se souvenait** de tout ce qu'il a appris!*
> Oh! If only he could remember everything he learnt!

- a polite alleviation of a request or recommendation:

> *Je **voulais** vous demander votre avis.*
> I would like to ask your advice.

THE PAST HISTORIC

The past historic expresses an accomplished action which happened at a well-defined moment in the past, differing from the imperfect which expresses duration or repetition:

> *On **entendait** sans cesse du bruit au grenier; on y **monta**.*
> We heard a constant noise coming from the attic; we went up.

The action of *"monter"*, considered as a limited event in time, contrasted with the duration of the noise being heard.
The past historic is in contrast with the present indicative, because it expresses an accomplished action at the moment of speaking:

> *Chacun sait que Christophe Colomb **découvrit** l'Amérique en 1492.*
> Everyone knows that Christopher Columbus discovered America in 1492.

THE PRESENT PERFECT

The present perfect expresses a finished action in the past at a time which is not necessarily precise:

> *Elle **a voyagé** souvent à l'étranger./* She has often travelled abroad.

■ PARTICULAR USES OF THE PRESENT PERFECT

– The present perfect can also be used to express a past action at a precise moment in time but where the moment in time is part of a time space in which the action has still not seen completion:

*Le xxe siècle **a vu** les premiers vols de l'homme dans l'espace.*

The 20th century saw the first space flights by man.

– The present perfect can also be used in the sense of the future perfect to express an action which will be finished in the near future:

***J'ai fini** dans cinq minutes.* / I'll have finished in five minutes.

– The present perfect replaces the future perfect in conditional clauses introduced by **si**:

*Si demain la fièvre n'**a** pas **baissé**, rappelez-moi.* / If the fever hasn't dropped by tomorrow, call me.

NOTE : In spoken French, the present perfect has now replaced the past historic.

THE PAST ANTERIOR

● The past anterior expresses an action which takes place immediately before another past action. It is most commonly used in phrases introduced by a conjunction of time (**quand, lorsque, dès que,** etc.):

*Quand elle **eut achevé** son discours, elle sortit de la salle.*

When she had finished her speech, she left the room.

● Sometimes, in a non-subordinate clause, the past anterior is used to express two actions in the past which happen in rapid succession:

*Il reçut un coup du poing, il **eut** vite **répondu**.* / Having taken a punch, he retaliated quickly.: in reality the act of response has taken place after the act of receiving.

THE PLUPERFECT

● The pluperfect expresses a past action which took place before another past action, but, unlike the past anterior, there could be a fairly long time span between the two actions:

*Il **avait connu** l'aisance; il était maintenant dans la misère.*

He had known good times; now he was destitute.

● The pluperfect expresses a customary or repeated action which happens before another past action:

*Lorsqu'elle **avait lu** un livre, elle en parlait toujours.*

When she had read a book, she always talked about it.

▓PARTICULAR USES OF THE PLUPERFECT

The pluperfect can also be used to express the following:

– in conditional clauses where the condition required for achieving an action has not been met.

> *Cet accident ne lui serait pas arrivé s'il **avait été** plus prudent.*
> He wouldn't have had this accident if he had been more careful.

– regret for a past action which didn't happen:

> *Ah! si vous **aviez pu** savoir!/*Oh! if only you'd known!

THE FUTURE PERFECT

The future perfect is used to express a future action which must or can happen before another future action:

> *Quand nous **aurons lu** ce paragraphe, vous pourrez sortir.*
> When we've read this paragraph, you'll be able to leave.

▓PARTICULAR USES OF THE FUTURE PERFECT

The future perfect can also be used as follows:

– to express a conjecture or supposition:

> *Elle est en retard: elle **aura eu** un empêchement de dernière minute./*She's late: she must have been held up at the last minute.

– to tone down, out of politeness, an expression related to a past event:

> *Vous vous **serez trompé**.*
> I'm afraid you've made a mistake.

– to express indignation:

> *Décidément, j'**aurai** tout **vu**!*
> Really, I've seen everything!

– to indicate, in historic narrative, a past action which is prior to another past action:

> *Les troupes de Montcalm étaient dispersées. Quand il **aura pu** les rassembler, il sera trop tard.*
> Montcalm's troops were scattered. When he had got them together again, it would be too late.

THE SUBJUNCTIVE MOOD

The subjunctive mood has two main uses:
• in subordinate clauses it depends on the syntax, its use being dependent on the verb in the main clause;
• in independent clauses, it depends on the intention of whoever is speaking.

MEANING AND USE OF THE SUBJUNCTIVE

● In independent or main clauses, the subjunctive expresses:

– orders: *Qu'elle **prenne** la voiture pour venir.*/Let her take the car to come.

– prohibitions: *Que rien **ne soit décidé** en mon absence.*/Don't decide anything in my absence.

– wishes: *Que vos vacances **soient** réussies!* Have a good holiday!

– suppositions: *Qu'un incident **survienne** et c'est la catastrophe.*/Any unforeseen incident and it's a disaster.

● In subordinate conjunctive clauses, the subjunctive is used when the verb in the main clause expresses:

– will: *Je veux que vous **écoutiez** avec attention.*/I want you to listen to me very carefully.

– doubts or fears: *Je ne crois pas qu'elle **vienne**. Je crains qu'il ne s'en **aperçoive** trop tard.*/I don't believe she's coming. I'm afraid he'll notice it too late.

– feelings: *Je suis heureux qu'elle **ait eu** beau temps.* / I'm pleased she's had good weather.

● In subordinate clauses which are conjunctive or relative (see page 153), the subjunctive can be used when the subordinate clause expresses the following ideas:

– aims: *Je lui montre la lettre afin qu'il **comprenne** toute l'affaire.* I am showing him the letter in order that he understands the whole affair.

– concessions: *Bien que la pièce **fût** médiocre, on ne s'ennuyait pas.* Even though the play was below par, we didn't find it boring.

– conditions: *Réglons cela, à moins que vous ne **vouliez** réfléchir.* Let's settle it, unless you want to think about it.

– consequences: *Ce n'est pas si compliqué qu'on ne **puisse** comprendre.* It is not so complicated that we can't understand.

SUBJUNCTIVE TENSES IN SUBORDINATE CLAUSES

In subordinate clauses the subjunctive tense depends on the tense of the verb in the main clause (sequence of tenses).

Main clause	Subordinate	Examples
present or **future**	**present** (present or future action)	*Je **doute** qu'elle **ait** assez d'énergie.* I doubt she has enough energy. *Demain j'**exigerai** qu'il se **taise.*** Tomorrow I will insist that he keeps quiet.
	past (past action)	*Je **doute** qu'elle **ait eu** assez d'énergie.* I doubt that she had enough energy. *Demain j'**exigerai** que tu **aies fini** pour cinq heures.* Tomorrow I will insist that you finish at five o'clock.
past or **conditional**	**imperfect** (simultaneous action)	*Je **voudrais** qu'il **eût** assez d'énergie.* I would've liked him to have had enough energy.
	pluperfect (preceding action)	*Je **craignais** qu'il ne **fût venu** pendant mon absence.* I was afraid that he had come when I wasn't here.

THE IMPERATIVE MOOD

The imperative expresses an order or a prohibition (*Regardez ces fleurs, ne les cueillez pas./* Look at these flowers, don't pick them.)

In the first and third person singular and plural, the present subjunctive replaces the imperative (*Qu'elle rentre avant huit heures!/Let her come back home before eight!*).

PARTICULAR USES OF THE IMPERATIVE

As well as orders and prohibition the imperative is also used to express:

– advice: *Ne vous **énervez** pas. **Attendez!** /* Don't get excited. Wait!

– wishes: ***Passez** de bonnes vacances vous et les vôtres. /* Have a good holiday, you and yours.

– suppositions: ***Ôtez** la virgule, le sens devient différent./*Remove the comma and you change the meaning.

– prayers: ***Faites**, ô mon Dieu, qu'il reconnaisse son erreur!/*O Lord, make him realize his mistake!

Sometimes the negative imperative of the verb ***aller*** followed by an infinitive is used in order to use someone not to do something.

> *N'**allez** pas **penser** que je vous soupçonne./*Don't go thinking I suspect you.

USE OF TENSE IN THE IMPERATIVE

● The present imperative expresses an order, request or prohibition bearing on the present or future:

> ***Versez**-moi à boire./Pour me a drink.*

> *Ne **viens** pas mardi, **téléphone**-moi./*Don't come Tuesday, phone me.

● The present imperative can also express a condition required for achieving the action expressed in the clause which follows it:

> ***Accepte** ma proposition et je me retire.*
> Accept my proposition and I withdraw.

> ***Parlez**-lui de politique, il ne vous écoute pas.*
> Talk to him about politics and he doesn't listen to you.

● The past imperative expresses an order (or a prohibition) which has to be carried out at a given moment in the future:

> ***Soyez levés** demain avant huit heures./Be up before eight o'clock tomorrow.*

THE CONDITIONAL MOOD

The conditional expresses an action or a state which depends on certain conditions for their achievement: *Si je le savais, je te le dirais volontiers.* / If I knew it, I would willingly tell it to you. (what is said depends on the degree of information I have).

The conditional can be used to express:

– imaginary events: *On se **croirait** en été.* / You'd think it was summer.;

– suppositions: *Au cas où vous **changeriez** d'avis, prévenez-moi.* / Let me know if you change your mind.;

– wishes: *J'**aimerais** aller à la mer cet été.* / This summer, I'd like to go to the seaside.;

– astonishment: *Elle **viendrait** samedi pour repartir lundi matin?* / She's coming Saturday and leaving Monday morning?

– uncertainty: *On **serait** sur la piste des coupables.* / We may be on the track of the culprits.;

– politeness: *Je **désirerais** que vous répondiez dès que possible.* / I would like you to reply as soon as possible. (less imperative than *"je désire que vous répondiez"*);

– indignation: *Et je **devrais** me taire!* / And I'll have to keep quiet!

CONDITIONAL TENSES

Tense	Meaning	Examples
present conditional	potential (possible action in the future)	*Si vous me donniez son adresse j'**irais** tout de suite la trouver.* If you gave me her address I would go and find her immediately.
	unreal present (action presently impossible)	*Si je ne vous savais pas étourdi, je vous **confierais** cette lettre.* If I didn't know you were absent-minded, I would trust you with this letter (but I know you are).
past conditional	unreal past (action which it was not possible to do)	*Si j'avais su que vous étiez à Lyon, je **serais allé** vous voir.* If I had known you were in Lyons, I would have gone to see you (but I didn't know).

THE CONDITIONAL USED AS THE FUTURE

The past or present conditional is used with the sense of the simple future or future perfect in subordinate clauses when the verb in the main clause (verbs of utterance or opinion) is in the past tense. This is referred to as "the future in the past".

Il affirme qu'il viendra.
He declares he's coming.

→ *Il affirmait qu'il viendrait.*
→ He declared he'd come.

Il affirme qu'il viendra dès qu'il aura terminé.
He declares he's going to come as soon as he's finished.

→ *Il avait affirmé qu'il viendrait dès qu'il aurait terminé.*
→ He had declared he'd come as soon as he'd finished.

THE INFINITIVE MOOD

The infinitive is a verbal form which expresses an action without any indication of person or number: *Nous avons vu l'orage venir, les nuages s'amonceler.* / We saw the storm coming, the clouds gathering.

The infinitive can also take the place of a noun with all its functions: *Elle consacrait plusieurs heures par jour à lire.*/She devoted several hours a day to reading. (= *à la lecture*); here, *"lire"* is the indirect object of *"consacrait"*.

TENSES IN THE INFINITIVE

● The present infinitive indicates an action taking place at the same time as the main verb:

> *Je l'entends* **chanter**. – *Je l'ai entendu* **chanter**.
> I heard him sing. – I have heard him sing.

● The past infinitive indicates an action which takes place before that of the main verb:

> *Après* **avoir rangé** *ses livres, il se prépare à aller en classe.*
> Having put away his books, he got ready to go to class.

PARTICULAR USES OF THE INFINITIVE AS A VERB

Among the particular uses of the infinitive as a verb in a sentence, distinction is made between the following uses:
– the infinitive as an order, acting as an imperative, expressing an order or prohibition (with the negative):

> **Agiter** *le flaçon avant de s'en servir.* **Ne pas exposer** *à l'humidité.*
> Shake the flask before using. Don't expose it to humidity.

– the infinitive of narration, acting as an indicative. Preceded by the preposition *de*, it indicates an action which follows on rapidly from what has just been said. This use is reserved for the language of literature:

> *Elle acheva son histoire, et tous* **de rire**.
> She finished her story and everybody laughed.

– the infinitive of exclamation, acting as an indicative, expressing surprise:

> *Moi, lui* **dire** *que je l'aime! Je n'oserais jamais!*
> Me, tell him I love him! I would never dare!

– the infinitive of deliberation expressing uncertainty:

> *Que* **faire**? *Qui* **croire**?
> What can be done? Who would you believe?

The infinitive used as a noun (substantive infinitive) has all the functions of a noun:

– subject: ***Promettre*** *est facile,* **tenir** *est difficile.* (*"promettre"* and *"tenir"* are both subjects of *"est"*)/Promising something is easy, to keep a promise is difficult.;

– logical subject: *Il est bon de **parler** et meilleur de **se taire**.* (*"parler"* and *"se taire"* are the logical subjects of *"est"*)/It's good to speak out, but it's sometimes better to keep quiet.;

– complement of the noun: *Je fus retenu par la crainte de le **vexer**.* (*"vexer"*, complement of the noun *"crainte"*)/I stopped for fear of hurting him.;

– complement of the adjective: *C'est une manœuvre très difficile à **faire**.* (*"faire"* complement of the adjective *"difficile"*)/It's a very difficult operation to do.;

– complement: *Votre devoir est d'**intervenir**.* (*"intervenir"*, complement of the subject *"devoir"*)/Your duty is to intervene.;

– direct object: *Elle aurait aimé vous **seconder** dans ce travail.* (*"seconder"*, direct object of *"aurait aimé"*)/She would have liked to help you with this work.;

– indirect object: *A-t-elle pensé à **envoyer** la lettre?* (*"envoyer"*, indirect object of *"a pensé"*)/Did she think to send the letter?;

– adverbial complement of objective: *Il ne sait que faire pour la **contenter**.* (*"contenter"*, adverbial complement of objective for *"ne sait que faire"*)/His only desire is to satisfy her.;

– adverbial complement of manner: *Elle passa devant moi sans me **saluer**.* (*"saluer"*, adverbial complement of manner for *"passa"*)/She passed in front of me without even saying hello.;

– adverbial complement of cause: *Pour **avoir** trop **mangé**, elle eut une indigestion.* (*"avoir mangé"*, adverbial complement of cause for *"eut"*)/ Having eaten too much, she had indigestion.;

– adverbial complement of means: *À force de **réclamer**, elle obtint satisfaction.* (*"réclamer"*, adverbial complement of means for *"obtint"*)/Due to asking, she got satisfaction.;

– adverbial complement of time: *Avant d'**avoir pu** me mettre à l'abri, je fus trempé.* (*"avoir pu"*, adverbial complement of time for *"fus trempé"*)/Before reaching shelter, I was soaken through.;

– adverbial complement of consequence: *Il est faible au point de **s'évanouir**.* (*"s'évanouir"*, adverbial complement of consequence for *"est faible"*)/He is weak and on the point of fainting.;

– adverbial complement of condition: *À **courir** après lui, je serais vite essoufflée.* (*"courir"*, adverbial complement of condition for *"serais essoufflée"*)/To run after him would soon make me breathless.;

– adverbial complement of concession: *Pour **être sévère** je n'en suis pas moins compréhensif.* (*"être sévère"*, adverbial complement of concession for *"suis"* [= *"bien que je sois sévère"*])./Even though I'm strict, it doesn't make me less understanding.

THE PARTICIPLE MOOD

The participle is a verb form having the value of a verb when expressing an action or a state, and the value of an adjective when relating qualitatively to a noun or pronoun. There is a present participle and a past participle.

THE PRESENT PARTICIPLE

The present participle is used as a verb or an adjective.

● **Proper present participle**: an invariable verb form often followed by a complement expressing an action currently taking place:

> Une meute **hurlant** de fureur s'acharnait sur la bête.
> A pack roaring with fury threw themselves on the animal.

● **Gerund**: an invariable verb form preceeded by the preposition **en**, expressing a circumstance of the main verb:

> **En prenant** l'escabeau, vous atteindrez le rayon.
> By taking the stepladder, you will reach the shelf.

● **Verbal adjective**: used as a variable qualifying adjective, expressing a quality:

> Vous avez des enfants obéissant**s**./You have obedient children.
>
> la meute hurlant**e** des chiens/the howling pack of the dogs

⚠ Sometimes the proper present participle and the verbal adjective are spelt differently, e.g.:

– present participle: *provoquant, fatiguant, vaquant, naviguant, négligeant*;
– verbal adjective: *provocant, fatigant, vacant, navigant, négligent.*

THE PAST PARTICIPLE

The past participle can be used both as a verb and an adjective.

● **Proper past participle**: a verb form often followed by a complement, expressing a past action or a present state:

> **Appliqués** à leur travail, ils ne nous avaient pas vus. (= étant appliqués)./Committed to their work, they had not seen us.

● **Verbal adjective**: used as a qualifying adjective:

> Marie est une élève **appliquée**./Marie is a committed pupil.

VERB AGREEMENT WITH THE SUBJECT

In the personal mood, the verb agrees with both the person and number of the subject. This agreement underlines the direct link between the two essential elements of the sentence: the noun group (or the replacement pronoun) and the verb group.

VERB AGREEMENT WITH THE SUBJECT

If the verb has only one subject, it agrees with the person and number of that subject:

Il *descend* *les escaliers.* *Les enfants* *jouent* *dans la cour.*

subject	verb		subject 3rd pers.	verb 3rd pers.
3rd pers.	3rd pers.		plur.	plur.
sing.	sing.			

He is coming downstairs. The children are playing in the yard.

Toi qui aimes tant te baigner, tu serais heureuse ici. (subjects: 2nd pers. sing.; verbs: 2nd pers. sing.)
You who like swimming so much, you will be happy here.

C'est moi qui suis votre nouvelle voisine. (subject: 1st pers. sing.; verb: 1st pers. sing.)
I'm your new neighbour.

SPECIFIC CASES WITH A SINGLE SUBJECT

● The verb is in the plural if the subject is **many** or **most** or an adverb of quantity accompanying the noun complement in the plural:

La plupart des invités étaient venus./Most of those invited had come.

Beaucoup des badauds s'arrêtaient./A lot of passersby stopped.

Bien des femmes riaient./A lot of women laughed.

Trop de gens criaient./Too many people were shouting.

● According to the nuance of meaning, the verb is in the singular or plural if the subject is an expression such as **un des... qui, un tiers, un quart**, or a collective noun followed by a complement in the plural:

C'est une des pièces qui constituent l'ensemble./It's one of the parts which form the whole thing.

*C'est **une** des pièces qui **est** essentielle à l'ensemble.* /It's one of the main parts of the whole.

*C'est **un des films** qui plaît or plaisent le plus au public.* /It's one of the movies which the public enjoys.

***Une foule d'admirateurs** l'attendait or l'attendaient à la sortie.* /There was a crowd of admirers waiting for her outside.

● When a pronoun-relative subject has a personal pronoun as an antecedent, the verb in the relative clause is put into the same person and number as the antecedent:

*Est-ce **toi** qui le leur as interdit?* /Is it you who forbade them to do it?

*C'est **nous** qui **avons** inventé cette histoire.* /we are the ones who made up this story.

Verb agreement with several subjects

● When a verb has several subjects, it is put in the plural:

***Le chêne et l'érable** masquaient la façade de l'hôtel.*
The oak and the maple masked the hotel facade.

● When a verb has different personal subjects, it is put in:

– 1st person plural if the subjects are in the 1st or 2nd person:

***Toi et moi** (= nous) nous **sommes** d'accord sur cette question.*
You and I, we agree about this point.

– 2nd person plural if the subjects are in the 2nd or 3rd person:

***Ta sœur et toi** (= vous) vous vous ressemb**lez** beaucoup.*
Your sister and you, you look very much alike.

⚠ When the verb has a polite "*vous*" as a subject, the past participle (and, possibly, the predicative adjective) is put in the singular:

*N'avez-**vous** pas été ému en l'entendant? Je **vous** croyais sensib**le**.*
Were you not moved by hearing him? I thought you were sensitive.

▮▮SPECIFIC CASES WITH SEVERAL SUBJECTS

● The verb can indifferently be put in the singular or the plural:

– if the subjects in the singular are linked by the conjunctions ***comme, ou, ni, ainsi, que***:

***Ni** lui **ni** sa femme n'entendit or n'entendirent sonner.*
Neither he nor his wife heard the ringing.

– if the subject is ***l'un et l'autre***:

***L'un et l'autre sont** tombés or **est** tombé.*
Both of them have fallen.

● The verb is in the plural when the subject is linked to another noun of the same importance by the preposition **avec**:

Ma sœur avec son ami sont allés au cinéma.
My sister and her friend have gone to the cinema.

If the second noun is incidental, the verb stays in the singular:

L'homme avec son chien march**ait** dans la forêt.
The man and his dog were walking in the forest.

● The impersonal verb, or the verb used in the impersonal sense, never agrees with the true subject, but stays in the 3rd person singular:

Il tomb**ait** de larges gouttes tièdes. ("gouttes" is the true subject; agreement with the apparent subject "il")./These were warm drops falling down.

● **C'est** can remain invariable with a plural noun or pronoun:

C'**est eux** or ce **sont eux** les coupables./They are the guilty ones.

C'ét**ait** or c'ét**aient** de **véritables festins**./It was a real feast.

⚠ When a verb has several subjects expressing a single general idea, it remains in the singular:

Dormir et manger **est** indispensable pour travailler.
Sleeping and eating are indispensable for work.

AGREEMENT OF THE PAST PARTICIPLE

The agreement of the past participle is one of the major difficulties in French. In effect, this agreement depends on the auxiliary, the nature of the complement and its position, and, for the reflexive verb, on the function of the pronoun.

PAST PARTICIPLE USED WITHOUT AUXILIARY

The past participle used without an auxiliary agrees in gender and number with the noun it relates to, as does the qualifying adjective with which it might be assimilated:

> Les **villas édifiées** sur la colline jouissent d'une vue étendue.
> The villas built on the hill enjoy an extensive view.

> Abandonn**ée** au bord de la route, une **voiture** accident**ée** rouillait.
> Abandoned by the roadside, a crashed car was rusting.

PAST PARTICIPLE CONJUGATED WITH "AVOIR"

RULE

The past participle conjugated with the auxiliary "avoir" (compound tense of active verbs) agrees in gender and number with the preceeding direct object:

> Vous avez **pris** la bonne **route**./ You have taken the right road.

> C'est la bonne **route que** vous avez **prise**./ This is the right road you have taken.

The participle remains invariable:

– if the verb has no direct object:

> Ils ont répond**u**./ They answered. (no direct object);

> Ils ont répond**u** sans retard./ They answered without any delay. ("sans retard": adverbial complement of manner);

> Ils ont répond**u** vite à notre lettre./ They quickly answered our letter. ("à notre lettre": indirect object);

– if the direct object comes after the participle:

> Nous avons mang**é des fruits**. Elle a re**çu** de bonnes **nouvelles**.
> We ate fruit. She received some good news.

132

■ FOLLOWED BY AN INFINITIVE

The past participle, conjugated with *"avoir"* and followed by an infinitive which is a direct object, remains invariable:

Vous auriez dû écouter. (*"écouter"*: infinitive as a direct object);

Vous auriez dû écouter nos conseils. /You should have listened to our advice. *les conseils que vous auriez dû écouter*/the advice you should have listened to.	(*"conseils"*: direct object of the infinitive *"écouter"*, not of the verb *"devoir"*).

This construction is found after verbs of perception (***voir, entendre, sentir***, etc.) and some verbs implying obligation or willingness, etc. (***laisser, faire, vouloir, devoir, pouvoir, omettre de***, etc.).

⚠ ● With the verbs ***voir, regarder, entendre, sentir***, and ***laisser***, the subject of the infinitive should not be confused with its direct object:

*J'ai entendu entrer **Odile**.* (= qu'Odile entrait): *"Odile"* is the subject of *"entrer"* and the direct object of *"ai entendu"*./I heard Odile come in.

*J'ai entendu féliciter **Odile**.* (= qu'on félicitait Odile): *"Odile"* is the direct object of *"féliciter"* and not the verb *"ai entendu"*./I heard Odile being congratulated.

● When the subject of the infinitive is placed before the past participle, the latter agrees in gender and number with the subject of the infinitive:

*la **cantatrice** que j'ai entend**ue** chanter:* *"cantatrice"* is the subject of the infinitive and preceeds the past participle *"entendu"* so there is agreement; *j'ai entendu qui? la cantatrice*, represented by *"que"*. *Elle chantait.*/the opera singer I heard singing.

On the contrary, in: *la romance que j'ai entend**u** chanter*/the love song I heard being sung, *"que"*, representing *"romance"*, is not the subject but the direct object of *"chanter"*. In this case, *"entendu"* remains invariable.

■ PRECEEDED BY THE PRONOUN "EN"

The past participle conjugated with the auxiliary *"avoir"* remains invariable if the direct object preceeding it is the pronoun *"en"*:
*J'ai cueilli des fraises dans le jardin et j'**en** ai mang**é**.* (j'ai mangé une partie des fraises)/I picked strawberries in the garden and I ate some of them.

■ PRECEEDED BY THE PRONOUN "L'" REPRESENTING A PROPOSITION

The past participle conjugated with *"avoir"* which has the neutral pronoun *"l'"* as a direct object (representing a whole proposition) remains invariable:

*La journée fut plus belle qu'on ne **l'**avait espér**é**:* *"l'"*, direct object of *"avait espéré"*, representing the proposition *"la journée fut plus belle"* (= le fait que la journée...)/The day was more beautiful than we could have hoped for.

The past participles *couru, coûté, pesé, valu, vécu* remain invariable when used in their true sense. They are intransitive:

> *La somme importante qu'a coûté ce pardessus*: true meaning; no agreement because there is no direct object (it's not possible to say: *a coûté quoi?* but: *a coûté combien?* "*somme*" is the adverbial complement of price)/The large sum this overcoat cost;

> *les vingt minutes que nous avons couru*/the twenty minutes that we ran: true meaning; no agreement because there is no direct object / (it's not possible to say: *couru quoi?* but: *couru pendant combien de minutes?* "*minutes*" is the adverbial complement of time).

⚠ Used in the figurative sense, these verbs are transitive and agree with the preceeding direct object:

> *les efforts qu'a coûtés cet examen*/the efforts this exam cost: figurative sense; agreement because: the exam has cost what? *des efforts* ("*efforts*" is a direct object);

> *les dangers que nous avons courus*/the dangers we've encountered: figurative sense; agreement because: we have encountered what? *des dangers* ("*dangers*" is a direct object).

■IMPERSONAL VERBS

The past participle of impersonal verbs or verbs taken as impersonal always remain invariable:

> *les deux jours qu'il a neigé*/the two days when it snowed: "*qu'*", representing "*days*", is the adverbial complement of time for "*a neigé*";

> *les accidents nombreux qu'il y a eu cet été*/the numerous accidents there's been this summer: "*qu'*", representing "*accidents*", true subject of "*a eu*".

PAST PARTICIPLE CONJUGATED WITH "ÊTRE"

■PASSIVE AND INTRANSITIVE VERBS

Conjugated with "*être*", the past participle of passive verbs and some intransitive verbs agrees in gender and number with the subject of the verb:

> La villa a été louée pour un mois. Les **hirondelles** sont part**ies.**
> | |
>   subject   participle
>   fem. sing.   in fem. sing.

The house has been let for a month. The swallows have left.

VERBS MAINLY PRONOMINAL AND PRONOMINAL IN THE PASSIVE SENSE

The past participle of verbs which are mainly pronominal or verbs which are pronominal in the passive sense, always conjugated with the auxiliary *"être"*, and agree in gender and number with the subject:

> *Ils se sont aperçus de leur erreur. Ces robes se sont bien vendues.*
> They noticed their error. These dresses have sold well.

REFLEXIVE AND RECIPROCAL PRONOMINAL VERBS

The past participle of reflexive and reciprocal pronominal verbs, always conjugated with the auxiliary *"être"*, follows the rules of past participles conjugated with the auxiliary *"avoir"* and agree in gender and number with the reflexive or reciprocal pronouns (*me, te, se, nous, vous*) if these pronouns are direct objects:

> *Elle s'est regardée dans la glace*: she looked at who? *"elle"* (represented by *"s'"*), *"s'"*, reflexive pronoun, is a direct object, so there is agreement.

> *Vous vous êtes battus dans la rue*: you beat who? *"vous"*, vous is a reciprocal pronoun, and a direct object, so there is agreement.

The past participle does not agree with the reflexive or reciprocal pronoun if the latter is an indirect object or a second object:

> *Ils se sont lavé les mains*: they washed who's hands? theirs (represented by *"se"*), *"se"* is a second object, so there is no agreement.

> *Nous nous sommes écrit*: we wrote to whom? us (= one to the other), *"nous"* is a second object, so there is no agreement.

⚠ If the direct object of the reflexive or reciprocal pronominal verb comes before the participle, the particple agrees with the direct object: *la jambe qu'il s'est tordue*/the leg that he twisted: *"qu'"* represents *"jambe"*, direct object of *"s'est tordue"*; *les injures qu'ils se sont adressées*/the insults that they've exchanged: *"qu'"*, represents *"injures"*, direct object of *"se sont adressées"*.

Adverbs

An adverb is an invariable word which modifies the meaning of an adjective, verb or another adverb: *Tu parles trop.*/You speak too much. Adverbs can be single words (*"bien"*, *"fort"*, *"toujours"*, *"là"* ...) or an adverbial phrase (*"tout de suite"*, *"à rebours"* ...). There are adverbs of manner, quantity, place, time, opinion (affirmation, negation), and interrogation. An adverb, like an adjective, can have a complement.

Adverbs of Manner

Adverbs of manner replace a complement of manner or modify the action expressed by the verb:

> *Il agit **bien**. Il chante **faux**. Elle récite **par cœur**.*
> He acts well. He sings falsely. She recites by heart.

These are:

– adverbs originating from Latin: *bien, mal, mieux;*
– adjectives used as adverbs: *juste, faux, clair;*
– adverbial phrases: *de bon gré, à gauche;*
– adverbs formed from adjectives using the suffix "-ment".

NOTES

1. Adverbs of manner can also have the meaning of adverbs of quantity:

> *Elle est **bien** insouciante.*/She is very carefree. (= *elle est très insouciante*).

2. Adverbs of manner can become nouns:

> *On peut escompter **un léger mieux** dans son état.*/ One can expect a slight improvement in his condition.: here, "*mieux*" is a noun preceded by an article and accompanied by an adjective.

ADVERBS OF MANNER WITH "–MENT"

Most of the adverbs of manner with -**ment** are formed by simply adding the suffix -**ment** to the feminine form of the adjective:

> *heureux – heureu**se** – heureu**sement**.*

EXCEPTIONS

1. Adjectives ending in -**ant** and -**ent** form their adjectives with -**amment** and -**emment**:

> *sav**ant** – sav**amment**; prud**ent** – prud**emment**.*

2. Some adjectives form their adverbs with -**ément:**

> *précis – précis**ément**; profond – profon**dément**.*

3. Adjectives ending in a vowel often lose the **-e** from the feminine form (sometimes replaced by a circumflex):

hardi – hardiment; assidu – assidûment; goulu – goulûment.

4. Some adverbs of manner have been constructed using a now extinct form or based on adjectives which only exist in old French form:

*bref – bri**èvement; sciemment**.*

5. Some adverbs with **-ment** are formed from a noun base:

*bête – bête**ment**; diable – diablement.*

NOTE : Adverbs of manner, just like adjectives, have comparatives and superlatives:

*Il réfléchit **plus** longuement. Il est vêtu **très** élégamment.*
He is thinking for a long time. He is dressed very elegantly.

*Elle va bien – elle va **mieux** – elle va **le mieux** du monde.*
She is well – she is better – she's in the best of health in the world.

ADVERBS OF PLACE

Adverbs of place have the sense of an adverbial complement of place. They are single words or adverbial phrases:

*Il chercha **partout** ses lunettes, mais ne les trouva **nulle part**.*
He looked for his glasses everywhere, but couldn't find them anywhere.

They express:
– the place where someone is or is going to:

là, où, ici, ailleurs, à droite, à gauche, dedans, derrière, dessous, dessus, dehors, quelque part, partout, tout, en, y...

– the place someone has come from:

d'où, d'ici, de là, de partout, d'ailleurs, de derrière...

– the place where someone has been through: *par où, par ici, par là, y...*

NOTES

1. The adverb *ici* identifies closeness; the adverb *là* identifies distance:

Ici on est à l'ombre, là le soleil est trop chaud.
Here we are in the shade, there, the sun is too warm.

2. The adverb **voici** (which can be considered as a verb or a preposition) signifies whatever is approaching or whatever follows on; **voilà,** whatever is further away or whatever precedes:

Voilà qui est fort bien dit; voici maintenant ce qu'il faut faire.
There is something that is very well said; here is now what has to be done.

3. *En* and *y* are also personal pronouns.

ADVERBS OF TIME

Adverbs of time have the sense of an adverbial complement of time. They are single words or adverbial phrases, expressing:

– the date or moment:	*désormais, hier, aujourd'hui, demain…*
– repetition:	*souvent, fréquemment, de nouveau…*
– duration:	*toujours, longtemps, pendant ce temps…*
– order of events:	*avant, après, ensuite, dès lors, alors…*

NOTE : Several adverbs of time can have comparatives and superlatives: *souvent, moins souvent, plus souvent, très souvent, le plus souvent.*

ADVERBS OF QUANTITY

Adverbs of quantity indicate a quantity or a degree: *Il y a **peu de** fruits cette année. Son mal est **moins** grave qu'il le dit.* /There's not much fruit this year. His sickness is not as bad as he says.
Adverbs of quantity can be:

– single words: *trop, suffisamment, assez, autant, aussi, si…*
– adverbial phrases: *à peine, à moitié, peu à peu…*

When they express degree, they can be followed by a subordinate preposition of comparison: *Elle est **aussi** aimable **que l'était sa mère**.*/She's as pleasant as her mother was.

ADVERBS OF OPINION

ADVERBS OF AFFIRMATION

Adverbs of affirmation are used to express, reinforce or to tone down an affirmation. They are single words (***oui, certes, évidemment***…) or adverbial phrases (***sans doute, peut-être***…):

> ***Oui**, j'essaierai. **Assurément** elle viendra. **Peut-être** se décidera-t-elle.*
> Yes, I'll try. Surely she'll come. Maybe she'll make up her own mind.

The adverb of affirmation ***si*** is used (in place of "*oui*") after a question posed in the negative:

> *N'as-tu pas compris? **Si**.*/ Didn't you understand? Yes.

ADVERBS OF NEGATION

Adverbs of negation are used to express negation under various forms. Essentially, they are the adverbs ***non*** and ***ne*** (reinforced or not by other adverbs).

● ***Non*** can express:
– a negative response to a question posed in the affirmative: *Fait-il froid ce matin? **Non**;*

– reinforcement of a negation: **Non,** *je ne partirai pas.* /No, I won't leave.
– a negation bearing on one word: *devoir* **non** *remis*/homework not handed in;
– two opposed groups: *Elle l'a fait involontairement,* **non** *par intérêt.*/She did it involuntarily, not out of interest.

● **Ne... pas** is the usual negation: *Elle* **n'**a **pas** *entendu.*/She hasn't heard. *Je* **ne** *sais* **pas.**/I don't know.

● **Ne... point** is the literary negation: *Tu* **ne** *m'as* **point** *répondu.*/You didn't reply to me.

● **Ne... goutte** is a negation used in one sole expression *"n'y voir goutte"*: *Il* **n'**y *voit* **goutte**; *il doit porter les lunettes.*/He can't see a thing; he should wear glasses.

● **Ne... plus** signifies *"ne... pas désormais"*: *Il* **ne** *sort* **plus** *de chez lui.*/He never goes out any more.

● **Ne... guère** signifies *"ne... pas beaucoup"*: *Je* **ne** *l'ai* **guère** *vue ces jours-ci.*/I've hardly seen her these last few days.

● **Ne... que** signifies *"seulement"*: *Je* **ne** *reste* **qu'**un instant./I'm only staying a moment. *Elle* **ne** *connaît* **que** *l'anglais.* /She only knows English.

● **Ne** is sometimes used alone, without **pas** or **point**:
– in some expressions: *Il y a plus d'un mois qu'il* **n'**a plu./It's more than a month since it has rained. *Je* **n'**ai que faire de vos conseils./I don't need your advice. **N'**était votre étourderie.../If you were not absent-minded...;
– avec **aucun, personne, rien, nul, ni**: *Il* **ne** *m'a* **rien** remis pour vous./He didn't give me anything for you;
– in the expression **que ne** signifying *"pourquoi ne pas"*: **Que ne** le faites-vous?/Why don't you do it?
– often after **si**: **Si** je **ne** me trompe, je l'entends./If I am not mistaking, I hear him.;
– often with the verbs **oser, pouvoir, savoir**. *Elle* **n'**osait l'interrompre./She didn't dare interrupt him.;
– in consecutive relative subordinates, where the principal is in the negative: *Il* **n'**y a pas de chagrin que le temps **n'**adoucisse./Time heals all wounds.

⚠ **Ne** can be used in phrases where there should not be negation because it is in an affirmative sense; this is called the "expletive *ne*"; it is found frequently:
– with verbs expressing fear (affirmative or interrogative phrases): *Je crains qu'il* **ne** *vienne.*/I'm afraid he will come. *Crains-tu qu'il* **ne** *vienne?*/Do you fear that he comes?; *Elle a peur qu'il* **ne** *soit trop tard.*/ She's afraid it'll be too late.;
– with verbs expressing difficulty, except **défendre**: *Tu empêcheras qu'elle* **ne** *s'éloigne.*/You will prevent her going away.;
– with verbs expressing doubt (negative or interrogative phrases): *Je ne doute pas qu'il* **ne** *se rétablisse.*/I've no doubt he will recover.;
– after **de peur que, avant que, à moins que**: *Préviens-la avant qu'il* **ne** *soit là.*/Warn her before he'll be here.;
– after **peu s'en faut, autre, autrement que**, or after the comparative **que**: *Il est moins habile que je* **ne** *pensais.* /He's not as skilful as I thought.

■DOUBLE NEGATION

Double negation can express:

– a toned down affirmation: *Elle **n**'a **pas** dit **non*** (= *elle a presque dit oui*).
    She didn't say no.

– a necessity: *Tu **ne** peux **pas ne pas** accepter* (=tu es
    obligée d'accepter)./You cannot not accept.

– an absolute affirmation: *Il **n**'est **pas sans** savoir* (= *il est absolument
    certain qu'il sait*).
    He's not without knowledging.

ADVERBS OF INTERROGATION

Adverbs of interrogation introduce questions which bear on:

– time: ***Quand** passera-t-elle nous voir?*/When is she coming to
    see us?

– place: ***D'où** revient-t-il?* /Where is he coming back from?

– manner: ***Comment** sait-il cela?*/How does he know that?

– cause: ***Pourquoi** ne m'en a-t-elle rien dit?* /Why did not she say
    anything to me?

– quantity: ***Combien** sont-elles?* / How much are they?

– price: ***Combien** veut-il de sa maison?* / How much does he
    want for his house?

⚠ The adverbs of interrogation ***est-ce-que***, in direct interrogation, and ***si***, in
indirect interrogation, only bear on the action or state expressed by the
verb: ***Est-ce** qu'il parti en voyage? Peux-tu me dire **si** elle est partie?* /Has
he left on a journey? Can you tell me if she's left?

NOTE : Do not confuse ***si***, the subordinate conjunction with ***si*** as an adverb
of interrogation, or ***si*** as an adverb of quantity, or ***si*** as an adverb of affirmation.

ADVERBIAL COMPLEMENTS

■DETERMINING COMPLEMENTS

Some adverbs can take a determining complement introduced by a preposition, commonly called an "adverbial complement":
*Conformément **à ses habitudes**, elle alla se coucher tôt.* / As usual, she
went to bed early. ("*habitudes*" is the adverbial complement of the adverb
"*conformément*");
*Il dit qu'il avait assez **de place** pour s'installer.* / He said he had enough
space to settle down. ("*place*" is the adverbial complement of "*assez*").

■COMPARATIVE AND SUPERLATIVE COMPLEMENTS

Adverbs of manner have, like the adjectives, comparative and superlative
complements: *Elle va mieux **qu'hier**. Il réagit plus bêtement **que toi**.*/She's
better than yesterday. He reacts more stupidly than you.

PREPOSITIONS

A preposition is an invariable word which joins a noun, pronoun, adjective, infinitive, or a gerund to another term (verb, noun, etc.) and establishes a link between the two. In the phrase *J'ai appris la nouvelle de sa mort par le journal.*/I learnt of his death by the newspaper.,

"de" establishes a link between *"nouvelle"* and *"mort"*; *"par"* establishes a second link, between *"J'ai appris"* and *"journal"*. *"Mort"* is a complement of the noun *"nouvelle"*; *"par le journal"* is the adverbial phrase of means of *"J'ai appris"*.

FORMS OF PREPOSITIONS

Prepositions can be:

– single words: *à, après, avant, avec, chez, contre, de, depuis, derrière, dès, devant, en, entre, envers, outre, par, parmi, pendant, pour, près, sans, sous, sur, vers…*
– former participles or adjectives: *attendu, concernant, durant, excepté, moyennant, passé, plein, suivant, supposé, touchant, vu…*
– prepositional phrases: *à cause de, afin de, à force de, à travers, au-dessus de, auprès de, d'après, de façon à, en dépit de, faute de, grâce à, hors de, jusqu'à, loin de, par rapport à…*

ROLE OF PREPOSITIONS

A preposition can introduce a complement:

– of a noun: *Elle est docteur en médecine.*/She's a doctor of medicine.: *"médecine"*, complement of the noun *"docteur"*;
– of a pronoun: *Aucun de ses amis n'est là.*/None of his friends are there.: *"amis"*, complement of the pronoun *"aucun"*;
– of an adjective: *Ce médicament est mauvais au goût.*/This medicine tastes terrible.: *"goût"*, complement of the adjective *"mauvais"*;
– of an indirect object: *Elle se souvenait de son enfance.*/She remembers her chidhood.: *"enfance"*, is the indirect object of *"se souvenait"*;
– of an adverbial phrase: *Il a été blessé à la tête.* / He's been wounded in the head.: *"tête"* is the adverbial complement of place for *"a été blessé"*;

⚠ A preposition also introduces words which are not complements but are:

– true subject: *Il est utile d'étudier.*/It's useful to study.: *"étudier"*, true subject of *"est utile"*;
– attributive: *Je le tiens pour un homme honnête.*/I take him for an honest man.: *"homme honnête"*, complement of the direct object *"le"*;

141

– attributive adjective: *Y-a-t-il quelque chose **de nouveau**?/* Is there anything new? *"nouveau"*, attributive adjective of *"quelque chose"*;
– apposition: *Connaissez-vous l'île **de Ré**?/* Do you know the Ile de Ré? *"Ré"*, appositon to *"île"*.

Meaning of prepositions

Some prepositions express only one relationship and introduce a single type of complement, e.g.:
– **durant** always introduces an adverbial phrase of time: ***Durant toute sa vie**, il a vécu ici./* He's lived here all his life.;
– **parmi** always introduces an adverbial phrase of place: *Choisis **parmi ces livres**. /* Choose from these books.

Other prepositions can establish several links:

– **avec**: – adverbial phrase of accompaniment: *Elle sort tous les jours **avec son chien**./* Everyday she's going out with her dog.;

  – adverbial phrase of manner: *J'avançais **avec prudence**./* I moved forward carefully.;

  – adverbial phrase of means: *Ils ouvriront **avec le double** de leur clé./* They'll unlock the door with a duplicate of their key.;

  – adverbial phrase of time: *Elle se lève **avec le jour**./* She gets up at daybreak.;

– **dans**: – adverbial phrase of place: *Il se repose **dans sa chambre**./* He is resting in his bedroom.;

  – adverbial phrase of time: *Elles viendront **dans trois jours**./* They'll come in three day's time.;

  – adverbial phrase of manner: *Elle vit **dans une certaine aisance**./* She is well-off enough.

● Lastly, other prepositions establish multiple links and play very varied roles; these are what are called "tool words" (*mots-outils*) in French; here are some examples of functions which can be introduced:

– **par**: – adverbial phrase of place: *Nous sommes passés en voiture **par Ottawa**./* We drove through Ottawa.;

  – adverbial phrase of time: *Elle se baigne **par tous les temps**./* She has a bath in all weathers.;

  – adverbial phrase of means: *Nous sommes allés à Lyon **par avion**./* We went to Lyon by plane.;

  – adverbial phrase of cause: *Il agit toujours **par intérêt**./* He always acts in his own interest.;

  – adverbial phrase of manner: *La bijouterie a été attaquée **par surprise**./* The jeweller's shop has been attacked by surprise.;

  – agent: *Elle a été nommée **par le ministre**./* She has been appointed by the minister.;

– **de**: – indirect object: *J'use **de mon droit**.*/I exercise my right.;

– adverbial phrase of place: *Nous arrivons **de Dakar**.*/We are arriving from Dakar.;

– adverbial phrase of time: *Elle travaille **de deux heures à six heures**.*/She works from two to six.;

– adverbial phrase of cause: *Elle meurt **de faim**.*/She starves to death.;

– adverbial phrase of manner: *Elle cite tous ses textes **de mémoire**.*/She quotes all her texts from memory.;

– adverbial phrase of means: *Elle me fit signe **de la main**.*/She waved to me.;

– noun phrase: *Il monte une salle **de spectacle**.*/He sets up a theater.;

– **à**: – indirect object: *Il a assisté indifférent **à cet incident**.*/He witnessed that incident unconcerned.;

– adverbial phrase of place: *Nous allons **à Rome**.*/We go to Rome.;

– adverbial phrase of objective: *Il tend **à la perfection**.*/He aims for perfection.;

– adverbial phrase of means: *Je pêche **à la ligne**.*/I fish with the rod.;

– adverbial phrase of manner: *Tu te portes **à merveille**.*/You carry yourself marvelously well.;

– adverbial phrase of price: *Ces places sont **à moitié prix**.*/These places are at half-price.

⚠ The prepositions **à** et **de** contract with the definite article (see "The article" p. 63).

REPETITION OF PREPOSITIONS

When several complements of the same word are coordinated or juxtaposed, the prepositions are generally repeated before each complement. But this usage is not strictly observed:

*Elle me reçut **avec** amabilité **et** même **(avec)** une certaine satisfaction.*
She received me with kindness and even a certain satisfaction.

⚠ The prepositions **à, de, en**, are never repeated in the following situations:

– in set phrases: ***En** mon âme et conscience, je le crois coupable.*/In my heart and soul, I consider him guilty.

– when the various complements refer to the same person or thing or form a whole: *Je m'adresse **au** collègue et ami.*/I am addressing the colleague and friend.;

– when the numeral adjectives are coordinated by **ou**;

– in enumerations where the whole forms a group: *La pièce est **en** cinq actes et dix tableaux.*/The play is in five acts and ten scenes.

Conjunctions

The conjunction is an invariable word or phrase which is used to link up two elements. If it links two words together it is a coordinating conjunction, like "*et*" in *aller et venir* / to come and go or *des roses et des œillets* / roses and carnations. If it links two clauses, it is a coordinating conjunction when the two clauses are of the same type (e.g. two relative clauses); it is a subordinating conjunction if it links a subordinate clause with another clause, on which it depends.

Coordinating conjunctions

Coordinating conjunctions are used to link two elements between them which, in principle, are of the same type (nouns, pronouns, adjectives, adverbs, verbs, clauses) and in the same way (subject, complement, attributive adjective, etc.). There are seven coordinating conjunctions, each one with specific uses:

et = liaison, addition:
Mes neveux et ma nièce sont partis en vacances.
My niece and nephews have gone on holiday.

ou = alternative:
Il faut persévérer ou renoncer tout de suite.
One needs to persevere or give up at once.

ni = liaison, alternative negative:
Il ne veut ni ne peut accepter (= *et ne peut*).
He neither wishes to nor can accept.
L'homme n'est ni ange ni bête.
Man is neither an angel nor an animal.

mais = opposition:
Ils ne sont pas là, mais il n'est que huit heures.
They're not there, but it's only eight o'clock.

or = argumentation or transition:
Tous les hommes sont mortels or Socrate est un homme, donc Socrate est mortel.
All men are mortal, now Socrate is a man, therefore Socrate is mortal.

car = explanation:
Ferme la fenêtre car il y a un courant d'air.
Shut the window because there's a draught.

donc = consequence, conclusion:
L'heure du train est proche, nous allons donc vous quitter.
The train will soon be leaving so we'll have to leave you.

NOTE : : Some adverbs can play the role of coordinating conjunctions, expressing:

– an alternative: *soit... soit, tantôt... tantôt;*
– an opposition: *cependant, pourtant, néanmoins, toutefois, au reste, en revanche, d'ailleurs;*

– an explanation: *en effet, c'est-à-dire;*
– a consequence: *c'est pourquoi, aussi, partant, par conséquent, par suite;*
– a conclusion: *enfin, ainsi, en bref;*
– a time element: *puis, ensuite.*

SUBORDINATING CONJUNCTIONS

Subordinating conjunctions link a subordinate clause to another clause on which it depends, and, in particular, to a main clause. These conjunctions express:
– a cause – **parce que, puisque**, etc.: **Puisque** *vous le voulez, je sors.* / Since it's what you want, I'll leave.;
– an objective – **afin que, pour que, de peur que**: *Enlevez cette pierre,* **de peur qu**'*on ne bute contre elle.* / Move that stone for fear someone stumbles over it.;
– a time element – **quand, lorsque, dès que, avant que**, etc.: **Quand** *elle sera là, dites-le-moi.* / When she's there, let me know.; **Dès qu'**il fera jour, nous partirons. / As soon as it's daylight we'll leave.; **Avant** qu'elle parte, prévenez-le. / Warn him before she leaves.;
– a concession – **bien que, quoique**: **Bien que** *cet échec fût grave, elle ne se découragea pas.* / Even though this setback was serious, she didn't lose courage.;
– a condition – **si, pourvu que, pour peu que**: *Je serai heureux d'accepter votre invitation,* **pourvu que** *ma présence ne* **soit** *pas pour vous une gêne.* / I'll be happy to accept your invitation, if my presence is not an embarrassment for you.;
– a comparison – **de même que, comme**: **Comme** *nous l'avions pensé, le chemin était très dur.* / As we had thought, the road was very hard.;
– a consequence – **tellement que, tant que**: *J'ai* **tellement** *crié* **que** *je suis enroué.* / I shouted so much I made myself hoarse.

PECULIARITIES OF SOME SUBORDINATING CONJUNCTIONS

● **Que** is a subordinating conjunction which can introduce:
– a subordinating object clause:

> *Chacun espère* **que** *vous reviendrez.*
> Everybody's hoping you'll come back.

– a subordinate clause of cause:

> *Il se tait, non* **qu'**il ignore les faits, mais par discrétion (= parce que).
> He's keeping quiet, not because he's ignoring the facts, but out of discretion.

– a subordinate clause of objective:

> *Cachons nous ici* **qu'**on ne nous voie pas (= afin qu').
> Let us hide here so that no one will see us.

– a subordinate clause of time:

> *Elle dormait encore* **que** j'étais déjà loin (= lorsque).
> She was still sleeping when I was already long gone.

– a subordinate clause of condition:

Qu'on m'approuve ou qu'on me blâme, j'irai (= *même si*).
Whether they approve of me or blame me, I'll go.

– a subordinate clause of comparison:

*Il est **plus** âgé qu'il ne paraît.*
He's older than he looks.

– a subordinate clause of consequence:

*Elle riait, **que** c'était un plaisir de la voir* (= *de sorte que*).
She laughed in such a way, it was a pleasure to see her.

NOTES

1. **Que** can be substituted with all other subordinate conjunctions from one subordinate clause to another:

*Comme il était tard et **que** tous avaient faim, on leva la séance.*
As it was late and as everybody was hungry, the session was closed.

Similarly **quand... et que...**; **si... et que**; **lorsque... et que...**

2. Do not confuse **que** as a coordinating conjunction and **que** as a relative pronoun (*le livre **que** je lis*/the book I'm reading), or **que** as an interrogative pronoun (***Que** dit-elle?*/What does she say?) and **que** as an adverb of quantity (***Que** c'est beau!*/How beautiful it is!).

● **Comme** can be a subordinating conjunction which introduces:
– a subordinate clause of cause:

***Comme** il pleut, nous restons* (=*puisqu'*). / Since it's raining, we are staying.

– a subordinate clause of comparison:

*Il est mort **comme** il a vécu.* / He died as he lived.

– a subordinate clause of time:

*Nous sommes arrivés juste **comme** elle partait* (= *quand*). / We arrived just as she was leaving.

 Comme can also be an adverb of quantity: *Comme il est intelligent!*/ How intelligent he is!

● **Si**, subordinating conjunction expressing condition/hypothesis: *Si vous veniez, je serais heureux.* /If you could come, I'd be very happy.

NOTE : In other situations **si** can be:

– an interrogative adverb: *Demandez-lui **s**'il nous accompagnera.*
                              Ask him if he'll come with us.

– an adverb of quantity: *Je ne suis pas **si** étourdie que vous le dites.*
                              I'm not as absentminded as you make me out.

– an adverb of affirmation: *Ne viendrez-vous pas? **Si!***
                              Aren't you coming? Yes!

INTERJECTIONS

An interjection is an invariable word which is used to express an emotion, an order or a noise: *Oh! le magnifique tableau!*/ What a beautiful painting!. *Hé! vous, là-bas, approchez!*/Hey! you there, come on! *Et patatras! le voilà à terre.*/Crash! On the ground he is! *Bravo! elle a réussi.*/Well done! She has succeeded. An interjection has no relationship with other words in the phrase and has no grammatical function. It is followed by an exclamation mark (!) or, sometimes, by a question mark (?).

VARIOUS INTERJECTIONS

An interjection can be a single word expressing:

surprise	*oh! ah?*	contempt	*fi!*
pain	*aïe!*	warning	*gare!*
doubt	*bah!*	seeking explanation	*hein?*
lack of concern	*baste!*	regret	*hélas!*
approval	*bravo!*	hesitation	*heu...*
need for silence	*chut!*	disgust	*pouah!*
a call	*eh! hé! ho! allô?*		

● Interjective phrases are formed with several words:

> *eh bien!* (request or exasperation); *tout beau!* (appeasement); *en avant!* (encouragement); *juste ciel! mon Dieu!* (amazement); *fi donc!* (contempt); *au secours!* (call for help).

● Words such as nouns, verbs, etc. are accidentally interjections, e.g.:

alerte!	= warning	**halte!**	
allons!		**silence!**	} = an order
courage!	} = encouragement	**miséricorde!**	= terror
ciel!	= amazement	**attention!**	= warning
diable!	= surprise		

● Onomatopoeic words reproduce certain sounds:
pan! vlan! clic! clac! patatras! pif! paf! cric! crac! bang!

NOTE : Expressions of greeting are considered as interjections:

> *Bonsoir*/good evening, *au revoir*/good-bye, *adieu*/farewell, *bonjour*/good morning, *salut*/hello, *à bientôt*/see you soon.

PART III
FROM THE PHRASE TO THE TEXT
Clauses

A sentence is made up of several clauses. In principle, each clause contains a nominal group and a verbal group, that is, a subject noun accompanied by determiners, objects, or a subject pronoun, a verb accompanied by objects or a complement. There are as many clauses in a sentence as there are verbs in the personal mood (indicative, conditional, subjunctive, and imperative). A sentence is called "simple" when it contains only one clause; it is called "complex" when it contains several clauses.

INDEPENDENT CLAUSES

In a sentence, a clause is "independent":

– when it expresses a complete idea by itself;

– when it does not depend grammatically on any other clause (even if its meaning is only explainable in relation to other clauses);

– when it has no dependent clause:

> *Cette nouvelle lui avait rendu courage.*/This news had given him courage. (An independent clause).

This sentence only contains one clause, which has a verb (*"avait rendu"*), a subject (*"cette nouvelle"*) and an object (*"courage"*).

COORDINATION AND JUXTAPOSITION OF INDEPENDENT CLAUSES

There can be several independent clauses in a sentence; they are said to be "coordinated" when they are linked by a coordinating conjunction, and "juxtaposed" when they are not linked to each other by a link word:

Cette nouvelle lui avait rendu courage	*et*	*il reprenait confiance.*
independent clause	coordinating conjunction	independent clause coordinated with the first clause

This news had given him courage and he was recovering his confidence.

Cette nouvelle lui avait rendu courage	*;*	*il reprenait confiance.*
independent clause	punctuation	independent clause juxtaposed

MAIN AND SUBORDINATE CLAUSES

Two clauses may not be linked to each other by a coordinating conjunction, but by a relative pronoun or an interrogative word. A clause is called a "subordinate clause" when it begins with a subordinating conjunction, a relative pronoun or an interrogative word, and "main clause" when it is completed by one or several subordinate clauses:

Elle avait retrouvé le courage	*dont elle avait fait preuve jusqu'alors.*
main clause	subordinate clause

She had recovered the courage she had shown until now.

COORDINATION AND JUXTAPOSITION OF MAIN AND SUBORDINATE CLAUSES

Two or more main clauses (or subordinate clauses) can be juxtaposed or coordinated just like independent clauses:

*Lorsque les enfants **furent montés** dans la voiture,* ‖ *que chacun* ***se fut*** *bien **installé**,* ‖ *Sylvain **s'aperçut*** ‖ *qu'il **avait oublié** la valise* ‖ *et **dut remonter** quatre à quatre.*

As soon as the children had got into the car, and everyone was settled, Sylvain noticed that he had forgotten the suitcase and he had to go back upstairs four at a time.

Lorsque *les enfants furent montés dans la voiture,*	subordinate conjunctive clause;
que *chacun se fut bien installé,*	subordinate conjunctive clause juxtaposed to the preceeding clause;
Sylvain s'aperçut	main clause;
qu'il avait oublié la valise	subordinated conjunctive clause;
et *dut remonter quatre à quatre*	main clause coordinated with [Sylvain s'aperçut].

FORM OF INDEPENDENT AND MAIN CLAUSES

Independent and main clauses can be:

– affirmative or negative: ***Je n'ai rien aperçu*** ‖ *qui fût inquiétant*
I saw nothing disturbing.

– interrogative: ***Qu'as-tu vu*** ‖ *qui puisse te troubler?*
What have you seen to worry you?

– exclamative: ***Quelle émotion a été la nôtre*** ‖ *quand nous l'avons revu!*
What emotion we enjoyed when we saw him again!

– interpolated or inserted: *Je vous invite,* ‖ ***dit-elle,*** ‖ *à venir diner chez nous.*
I'm inviting you, she said, to come and eat at home with us.

ELLIPTICAL CLAUSES

In principle, a clause is made up of a verb and a subject. When the verb or the subject is omitted, the independent, main or subordinate clauses are called "elliptical clauses".

● **Ellipsis of a subject in coordinated and juxtaposed sentences, in the imperative, etc.**

> *Il s'arrêta,* puis repartit sans mot dire .   *Viens par ici.*
>
> independent elliptical clause
> (the subject *"il"* is omitted)

He stopped, then left without saying anything.   Come here.

● **Ellipsis of the verb in response to questions, orders, etc.**

> *Lui avez-vous donné rendez-vous?* Oui, demain à quatre heures .
>
> independent elliptical clause
> (*"je lui ai donné un rendez-vous"* is omitted)

Did you give him a rendez-vous? Yes, tomorrow at four o'clock.

> *Regardez l'inscription; on y lit: "* Défense d'afficher *".*
>
> independent elliptical clause

Look at the sign; it says: Don't stick bills.

In this clause, the verb is omitted (*il est fait défense d'afficher*); sometimes this type of clause is called a "noun phrase".

● **Ellipsis of the verb in comparative subordinate clauses:**

> *Il pense* comme moi ./He thinks the same as me.
>
> elliptical subordinate clause
> (*"je pense"* is omitted: *comme moi je pense*)

NOTE : This sentence can also be considered as consisting of one clause and "moi" be analysed as a comparative object of "pense".

⚠ Elliptical clauses must not be confused with:
– interrupted clauses (followed by suspension points):

> *Si jamais tu touches à mes papiers...*/If ever you touch my papers...

– exclamative clauses:

> *Ô rage! ô desespoir! ô vieillesse ennemie!* (Corneille)

– words in apostrophe:

> ***Les petits****, venez!*/Come, Little ones!

– interjections:

> ***Attention!*** *vous allez trop vite.*/Be careful! you're going too fast.

SUBORDINATE CLAUSES

The subordinate clause completes or modifies the meaning of a clause (main or subordinate) on which it depends. In the sentence *Je l'ai rencontré alors que je sortais de chez moi.*/I met him as I was leaving home., there are two clauses: *je l'ai rencontré,* main clause, *alors que je sortais de chez moi,* subordinate clause which adds an idea of time to the main clause.

NATURE OF SUBORDINATE CLAUSES

The subordinate clause can be introduced by a relative pronoun, a subordinating conjunction or by the interrogative (adverb, pronoun, adjective); the following distinctions being made:

– the relative clause:

Je n'ai pas lu le livre ‖ **dont vous me** parlez/I haven't read the book you're talking about: *"dont"*, relative pronoun, introducing the relative clause;

– object and adverbial clauses:

Il raconte ‖ **qu'il a été le témoin d'un terrible accident**./He's saying that he has been the witness of a terrible accident.: the conjunction *"que"*, introduces the object clause;

Elle est arrivée ‖ **alors qu'on ne l'attendait plus**./She arrived when no one expected her anymore.: the conjunction *"alors qu' "* introduces the adverbial clause;

– indirect interrogative clause:

Je lui disais ‖ **combien cette dent me faisait souffrir**./I told him how much I was suffering with this tooth.: the interrogative adverb *"combien"* introduces the indirect interrogative clause.

It is quite possible that subordinating clauses are introduced without a subordinating word (conjunction, relative or interrogative). This is the case with infinitive and participial clauses (see later).

FUNCTION OF SUBORDINATE CLAUSES

The function of subordinate clauses depends on their nature and the role they play in the sentence:

– relative clauses are either noun complements or the complement of antecedent pronouns;
– subordinate conjunctives can be a subject, complement, object or adverbial phrase.

Relative Clauses

Relative clauses are introduced by relative pronouns. They complete a noun or pronoun expressed in a preceeding clause, which is called an "antecedent". In the sentence *J'allais contem-* *pler le soleil qui se couchait sur la mer.*/I went and gazed at the sun setting on the sea.; *"soleil"* is the antecedent; *"qui"* introduces the relative clause.

Function of relative clauses

A relative clause complements the antecedent:

> *Cadet Rousselle a trois maisons **qui n'ont ni poutres ni chevrons**.*/Cadet Rousselle has three houses which have neither beams nor rafters.: relative clause, complement of the antecedent *"maisons"*.

⚠ The antecedent needs not be expressed. Then the relative clause has an indeterminate meaning (= *quiconque*/whoever):

> ***Qui agit ainsi** est digne de mon estime.*/Whoever acts thus deserves my respect.: *"qui agit ainsi"*: relative clause, complementing the antecedent *"celui"* which is not expressed.

NOTE : This clause can also be interpreted as the subject of the main verb *"est"*.

Mood of relative clauses

● The relative clause is generally in the indicative: *On était suffoqué par une odeur ‖ **qui prenait** à la gorge.*/We were choked by a smell which got in the throat.

● It is in the subjunctive:
– when it expresses an objective: *Trouvez un ami ‖ **qui devienne** votre confident.* (= *pour devenir*/to become)./Find a friend who can become your confidant.
– when indicating a consequence: *Il n'était pas de visage ‖ **qui exprimât** mieux la bonté* (= *tel qu'il pût mieux exprimer la bonté*)./There was no face which might better reveal kindness.
– after **le seul**, **le dernier**, **le premier** or a relative superlative: *Vous êtes le seul ‖ **à qui je puisse** demander ce service.*/ You're the only one I can ask for this service.

● It is in the conditional when it expresses possibility: *La personne ‖ **qui le rencontrerait** ‖ devrait aussitôt le prévenir.*/The person who happens to meet him should warn him immediately.

NOTE : A relative clause can also be in the infinitive: *Je ne voyais alors personne ‖ **à qui demander** ma route.*/I could see nobody about to ask the way.

Noun clauses

Subordinate clauses which are true subject or object of the main verb, or complement of the subject of this same verb, are called noun clauses. They can be introduced by a conjunction, an interrogative word (indirect interrogative noun clause), or be completed with no subordinate word (dependent clause in the infinitive).

Noun clause as subject of the main verb

The subject clause introduced by the conjunction *que* can be the true subject of an impersonal verb (or of a verb phrase having the meaning of an impersonal verb). It answers the question *"qu'est-ce qui"*/who/what is it that?:

> *Il est vraisemblable* ‖ *qu'il sera reçu à son examen.*/It is very likely that he will pass his exam.: *qu'est-ce qui est vraisemblable? "qu'il sera reçu à son examen"*, noun clause, true subject of *"est vraisemblable"*;

> *Qu'elle vienne demain* ‖ *me surprendrait.*/It would surprise me if she comes tomorrow.: *"qu'elle vienne demain"*, subject of *"surprendrait"*.

Noun clause as object of the main verb

A noun clause introduced by the conjunction *que* can be object of the verb in the main clause. It answers the question *"quoi?"*/what?. It is found after verbs of:

– declaration (*dire*/to say):
Elle affirme ‖ *que tout est en ordre.*
She declares that everything is in order.

– opinion (*penser*/to think):
Elle estime ‖ *qu'il faut le prévenir.*
She reckons we'll have to warn him.

– perception (*entendre*/to hear):
Tu vois ‖ *que ton devoir est de rester.*
You see that it is your duty to stay.

– willingness (*vouloir*/to want):
Je veux ‖ *qu'on soit sincère.*
I want us to be sincere.

– order/interdiction:
(*ordonner*/to order)
J'interdis ‖ *qu'on lui parle.*
I forbid anyone to speak to him.

– obstacle :
(*empêcher*/to prevent)
Elles ont empêché ‖ *qu'elle me rejoignit.*
They prevented her from joining me.

– fear (*craindre*/to fear):
Je crains ‖ *qu'elle ne puisse pas accepter.*
I'm afraid that she can't accept.

Noun CLAUSE AS COMPLEMENT OF THE SUBJECT OF THE MAIN VERB

A noun clause introduced by *que* can be subject of a main clause after such expressions as: *l'ennui est, le malheur est, le fait est*:

> *La vérité est* || *qu'il a fait face à la situation avec détermination.*/ The truth is that he faced up to the situation with determination.: the noun clause *"qu'il a fait face à la situation avec détermination"* is complement of the subject *"vérité"*.

Mood OF SUBJECT OR OBJECT NOUN CLAUSES

Subject or object noun clauses are generally in the indicative mood:

> *Il est vrai* || *qu'ils se sont parfaitement entendus.*
> It's true that they got along really well.

NOTE:
1. The subject or object noun clause is often in the subjunctive mood when the main clause is negative or interrogative:

> *Il n'est pas vrai* || *qu'ils se soient parfaitement entendus.*
> It's not true that they got along really well.

> *Est-il imaginable* || *Qu'elle ne réussisse pas son examen?*
> Is it possible to imagine that she won't pass her exam?

2. The subject or object noun clause is in the subjunctive after verbs expressing desire, doubt, fear, willingness:

> *Je désire* || *qu'elle revienne.*/I want her to come back.

Noun CLAUSES IN THE INFINITIVE

The verbs *voir, regarder, entendre, sentir* et *laisser* (more rarely *dire, croire* and *savoir*) can be followed by an object noun clause of which the verb in the infinitive is accompanied by a subject:

> *J'entends* || *Pierre chanter dans la pièce voisine.*/I hear Pierre singing in the next room.: the infinitive *"chanter"* has the subject *"Pierre"*; *"Pierre chanter dans la pièce voisine"* is a subordinating infinitive, the complementary object of *"entends"*.

⚠ To be an infinitive clause, the infinitive has to have an expressed subject which, at the same time, is a direct object of the verb in the main clause. Thus, in the following example: *J'entends chanter dans la pièce voisine,* there is no infinitive clause; *"chanter"* is an infinitive without a subject, and is the direct object of *"entendais"*, as is *"un chant"* in the sentence: *J'entends un chant dans la pièce voisine.*

INTERROGATIVE CLAUSES

An independent clause, or a main clause, can be in the interrogative form. In which case, it starts with an interrogative word (pronoun, adjective, adverb) or the construction involves an inversion (in colloquial French usually), and is followed by a question mark: *Pourquoi n'êtes-vous pas venu?* (independent interrogative clause)/Why didn't you come?; *Comment a-t-elle pu oublier* (main interrogative clause) *ce que je lui avais dit?* (subordinate clause)/How could she forget what I had told her?.

INDIRECT INTERROGATION

Instead of asking a question directly, verbs such as **demander, savoir, ignorer**, etc. can be used as go-betweens. The clause then becomes an indirect interrogative subordinate clause, starting with an interrogative word (adjective, pronoun, adverb). It is not followed by a question mark:

Je lui ai demandé ‖ ***s'il avait été malade.***/I asked him if he had been ill.: *"s'il avait été malade"*, indirect interrogative subordinate clause, introduced by the interrogative adverb *"s'"* (elided *"si"*);

Dis-moi ‖ ***qui tu hantes,*** *je te dirai* ‖ ***qui tu es.***/Tell me who you haunt and I'll tell you who you are.: *"qui tu hantes"* and *"qui tu es"*, indirect interrogative subordinate clauses, introduced by the interrogative pronoun *"qui"*.

FUNCTION OF THE INDIRECT INTERROGATIVE SUBORDINATE CLAUSES

An indirect interrogative subordinate clause is generally object, or more rarely subject, of the main clause:

Je voudrais bien savoir ‖ ***quel était ce jeune homme,*** ***Si c'est un grand seigneur et*** ‖ ***comment il se nomme.***
I would like to know who this young man was, If he is very generous and what is his name (Faust's libretto, Gounod's opera): *"quel était ce jeune homme, Si c'est un grand seigneur et comment il se nomme"* are indirect interrogative clauses, and object of *"savoir"*;

Quelle est son intention ‖ *reste un mystère pour nous.*/What he intends to do is still a mystery for us.: *"Quelle est son intention"*, indirect interrogative clause, subject of *"reste"*.

An indirect interrogative clause is often introduced by the interrogative adverb ***si***, introducing a conditional subordinate clause.

155

MOOD IN INDIRECT INTERROGATION

An indirect interrogative subordinate clause can be in different moods according to the sentence:

– indicative: *Nous ne savons pas* ‖ *quands nous le verrons.*/We don't know when we are going to see him.

– conditional: *Je me demande* ‖ *qui pourrait m'aider à repeindre.*/I'm wondering who might help me to repaint.

– infinitive: *Elle ne sait* ‖ *à qui s'adresser.*/She doesn't know who to talk to.

SUBORDINATE ADVERBIAL CLAUSES

Subordinate adverbial clauses indicate the circumstances surrounding, specifying, determining, motivating or explaining an action. They can be either conjunctive subordinate clauses, starting with a subordinating conjunction, or participial subordinate clauses.

SYNTACTIC FUNCTIONS OF ADVERBIAL CLAUSES

A subordinate adverbial clause plays the same syntactical role and has the same functions as any adverbial clause:

Je suis arrivé quand le spectacle commençait. /I arrived when the
        | show was starting.
    subordinate adverbial clause of time

This subordinate clause can be replaced by an adverbial complement of time: *au début du spectacle.*

TYPES OF SUBORDINATE ADVERBIAL CLAUSES

● Distinction is made between seven types of subordinate adverbial clauses. They express:

– time: time subordinate clause, also called "temporal clause";
– cause: causative subordinate clause (causal clause);
– objective: subordinate clause of purpose;
– consequence: consecutive subordinate clause;
– concession or opposition: concessive subordinate clause;
– condition: conditional subordinate clause;
– comparison: comparative subordinate clause.

● Some subordinate clauses fit badly into those seven sorts of subordinate adverbial clauses, so the following types are also referred to:

– subordinate clause of manner, introduced by **comme**, **sans que**: *Faites* || **comme vous pourrez.**/Do what you can.; *Il s'est absenté* || **sans que je le sache.**/He's gone out without my knowing it.
– subordinate clause of addition, introduced by **outre que**, **sans compter que**: **Outre que c'est cher**, || *c'est d'une qualité médiocre.*/Besides being expensive it is of mediocre quality.
– subordinate clause of exception, introduced by **sauf que**, **excepté que**: *Vous avez raison* || **sauf que votre hypothèse est peu probable.**/You are right except that your hypothesis is not very likely.

NOTE : Clauses introduced by **où** as a relative without an antecedent functioning as an adverb can be interpreted as subordinate adverbial clauses of place: *Qu'il aille* || **où il voudra.**/Let him go where he likes.

Subordinate Clauses of Time

A subordinate clause of time indicates the circumstances which preceed, follow or accompany the action of the main clause. It answers the questions *quand? depuis quand?*, etc.: *Quand le chat n'est pas là, les souris dansent/*When the cat's away the mice will play. *Les souris dansent quand? "quand le chat n'est pas là":* conjunctive subordinate clause, adverbial phrase of time of *"dansent".*

Various forms

The action indicated in the main clause can occur before (anteriority), after (posteriority) or during (simultaneity) the action expressed by the verb in the subordinate clause.

A subordinate clause of time can be in the indicative or subjunctive mood, following the subjunctive which introduces it.

Conjunctions	Moods	Examples
avant que, jusqu'à ce que, en attendant que	subjunctive	*Avant que le jour fût levé,* ‖ *les chasseurs partirent avec leurs chiens.* Before the rise of dawn, the hunters had left with their dogs.
après que, sitôt que,	indicative	*Après que vous aurez sonné à la porte trois fois,* ‖ *on vous ouvrira.* After you've rang the doorbell three times, someone will let you in.
tandis que, tant que, pendant que, comme	indicative	*Tant que la pluie tombera,* ‖ *nous ne pourrons sortir.* As long as it's raining, we won't be able to go out.
lorsque, quand, alors que	indicative	*Lorsque l'accident se produisit,* ‖ *elle traversait la rue.* She was crossing the road when the accident happened.
dès que, depuis que, aussitôt que	indicative	*Dès que vous aurez terminé,* ‖ *vous me préviendrez.* As soon as you've finished, let me know.

OTHER TIME EXPRESSIONS

The idea of time can also be expressed by:

● **a noun** as an adverbial phrase of time introduced by the prepositions *"avant"*, *"après"*, *"dès"*, *"depuis"*, etc., or without a preposition:

Il est debout `chaque matin` `dès 6 heures` .

adverbial complement   adverbial complement
of time without a   of time with a
preposition   preposition

He rises at six every morning.

● **an infinitive** as an adverbial phrase of time introduced by the prepositions *"avant de"*, *"après"*, *"au moment de"*, etc.:

Au moment de partir, un incident nous retarda.
Just when we were leaving, an incident held us up.

SUBORDINATE CAUSATIVE CLAUSES

A subordinate causative clause indicates the reason for the accomplished action expressed in the main clause (or in a clause on which this subordinate clause depends). It answers the question: *"pourquoi?"*/ why?, *"à cause de quoi?"*/ because of what?. *Allez jouer dans le jardin puisque la pluie a cessé.*/ Since the rain has stopped, go and play in the garden. *"Puisque la pluie a cessé"*, subordinate conjunctive clause, adverbial phrase of cause of *"allez jouer"*.

VARIOUS FORMS

Conjunctions	Moods	Examples
parce que, puisque, comme, vu que, attendu que, sous prétexte que, du moment que, outre que	indicative or conditional	*Comme tu a faim,* ‖ *prends cette tartine de confiture.*/As you're hungry, take this toast with jam. *On l'a arrêté* ‖ *sous prétexte qu'il aurait jeté des pierres.*/He was arrested under the pretext that he would've thrown stones.
non que, non pas que, ce n'est pas que	subjunctive	*Ce n'est pas que je veuille vous renvoyer,* ‖ *cependant il se fait tard* ‖ *et la nuit va tomber.*/It's not because I want to see the back of you, it's getting late however, and night is falling.

OTHER CAUSATIVE EXPRESSIONS

The idea of cause can also be expressed by:

● **a noun** as a causative adverbial phrase, with the prepositions or prepositional phrases *"à"*, *"d'"*, *"pour"*, *"grâce à"*, *"en raison de"*, etc.:

Faute de patience, *elle ne réussit pas à le calmer.*/She couldn't
⊦   calm him down because she lacked patience.
causative adverbial clause
for *"réussit"*

● **a participle in apposition**: *L'homme, **pressé**, était reparti.* (= *parce qu'il était pressé*)/The man, in a hurry, had left him again.

● **an infinitive** as a causative adverbial phrase, with most prepositions:

J'étais exaspéré d'avoir attendu *si longtemps.*/I was furious at having
⊦   had to wait so long.
causative adverbial clause
for *"étais exaspéré"*

● **a relative clause in the indicative mood**: *Cette personne* ‖ *qui a beaucoup voyagé* ‖ *pourra vous renseigner.*(= *parce qu'elle a beaucoup voyagé*)/This person, who has travelled a lot, will be able to help you.

SUBORDINATE CLAUSES OF PURPOSE

A subordinate clause of purpose indicates the purpose or intention for the accomplished action expressed in the main clause (or in a clause on which this subordinate clause depends). It answers the question: *"dans quel but?"* *Afin que les choses soient bien claires,* || *je vous rappelle mes propositions.*/To make it perfectly clear, I remind you of my proposals. *"Afin que les choses soient bien claires"*, subordinate conjunctive clause, adverbial phrase of purpose of *"rappelle"*.
Le chien aboie à la porte || *pour qu'on lui ouvre.*/The dog barks in front of the door for someone to open it. *"pour qu'on lui ouvre"*, subordinate conjunctive clause, adverbial phrase of purpose of *"aboie"*.

VARIOUS FORMS

Conjunctions	Moods	Examples
afin que, pour que, que	subjunctive	*Il faut vérifier chaque détail,* || *afin que tout aille bien.* Every detail will have to be checked so that all goes well.
de crainte que, de peur que	subjunctive	*Fermez la fenêtre,* || *de crainte que le petit ne prenne froid.* Shut the window, for fear the little one catches cold.

OTHER PURPOSE EXPRESSIONS

The idea of purpose can also be expressed by:

● **a noun** or **a noun group** has an adverbial phrase of purpose, and preceeded by a preposition: *Elle est sortie* **pour sa promenade quotidienne.**/She's out for her daily walk;

● **an infinitive** as an adverbial phrase of purpose, preceded by the following prepositions or prepositional phrases *"pour"*, *"afin de"*, *"en vue de"*, *"dans la crainte de"*, etc.: *Je n'avais pas répondu,* **de peur de le mettre en colère.**/I didn't reply for fear he would be angry;

⚠ The infinitive as an adverbial phrase of purpose must have the same subject as the main verb.

● **a relative clause in the subjunctive mood**: *Appelez un taxi* || **qui me conduise à la gare**. (= *pour qu'il me conduise*)/Call a taxi to get me to the station.

161

SUBORDINATE CONSECUTIVE CLAUSES

A subordinate consecutive clause indicates the result obtained or possible thanks to the action expressed in the main clause or in a clause on which the subordinate clause depends. It answers the question: *"en amenant quelle conséquence, quel résultat?"*.

Il agit de telle manière || *que personne n'eut plus confiance en lui.* He behaved in a way which led to what result? The fact that no one trusted him anymore is a conjunctive subordinate clause, a consecutive adverbial phrase of *"agit"* (here *"agir"* = to behave).

VARIOUS FORMS

Conjunctions	Moods	Examples
de telle sorte que, de telle manière que, au point que, si bien que	indicative	*L'accident fut brutal,* || *au point que nul ne put en établir les circonstances exactes.* The accident was violent, to the point that the exact circumstances couldn't be established. *La chétive pécore s'enfla si bien* || *qu'elle creva (La Fontaine).* The scrawny goose swelled so much that it blew up.
que signalled in the main clause by *tel*, or a quantitative adverb: *si, tant, tellement*, etc.	indicative or conditional	*Le bruit devint si intense que l'on dut fermer la fenêtre.* The noise got so loud we had to shut the window. *Il pleut tant* || *qu'on peut craindre une inondation.* Ii is raining so hard we're frightened there will be flooding.
de façon que, sans que, en sorte que, de manière que, trop (assez)... pour que	subjunctive	*Approche,* || *de façon qu'on te voie.* Come closer so that we can see you. *Il pleut trop* || *pour qu'on puisse aller se promener.* It's raining too hard to go walking.

⚠ When the main clause is negative or interrogative, the subordinate consecutive clause is in the subjunctive mood:

Elle n'est pas si naïve || *qu'elle n'ait pas compris l'allusion.* She's not that naive she didn't understand the allusion.

OTHER CONSECUTIVE EXPRESSIONS

The idea of consequence can also be expressed by:

● **an infinitive** preceeded by the prepositions or prepositional phrases *"à"*, *"assez... pour"*, *"trop... pour"*, *"de façon à"*, *"en sorte de"*, *"au point de"*, etc.:

> *Elle n'est pas partie **assez** vite pour gagner cette course.*
>
> consecutive adverbial clause
> for *"n'est pas partie"*

She didn't start quickly enough to win this race.

● **a relative clause in the subjunctive:**

> *Il est le dernier* ‖ *à qui nous puissions faire appel*.

He's the last one we could turn to for help.

SUBORDINATE CONCESSIVE CLAUSES

A subordinate concessive clause (sometimes called an opposing or restrictive clause) indicates something which would have prevent the fact or the action expressed in the main clause from being achieved. It answers questions such as *"en dépit de quoi?"*, *"malgré quoi?" Bien qu'il fût parti en retard, il a réussi à me rejoindre. /* Even though he left late, he managed to catch up with me. *Il a réussi à me rejoindre en dépit de quoi? "bien qu'il fût parti en retard"*, a conjunctive subordinate clause, concessive complement of *"Il a réussi à me rejoindre"*.

VARIOUS FORMS

Conjunctions	Moods	Examples
quoique, bien que, loin que, encore que, malgré que	subjunctive	*Elle était généreuse ‖ quoiqu'elle fût économe.* She was generous even though thrifty.
quelque... que, si... que used with an adjective or an adverb	subjunctive	*Quelque étonnant que cela paraisse, ‖ je ne m'aperçus de rien.* However amazing it seems, I didn't notice anything.
quelque... que with a noun before *quelque*	subjunctive	*Quelques objections qu'on lui opposât, ‖ il ne se décourageait pas.* Whatever objections we put to him, they didn't put him off.
même si, sauf que	indicative	*Même si ma vie était en jeu, ‖ je n'hésiterais pas.* Even if my life was on the line, I wouldn't hesitate.
quand même, lors même que	conditional	*Quand bien même il aurait eu raison, il devait céder.* Even though he had been right, he was forced to give in.

NOTE : The two last groups can also be considered as introducing conditional clauses.

OTHER CONCESSIVE EXPRESSIONS

The idea of concession can also be expressed by:

● **a noun** complement introduced by such prepositions as *"malgré"*, *"en dépit de"*, etc.:

> En dépit du sable *qui l'aveuglait, elle continua de marcher.*
>
> concessive adverbial clause
> of *"continua de marcher"*
>
> In spite of being blinded with sand, she carried on walking.

● **an infinitive** as a complement introduced by prepositions such as *"pour"*, *"loin de"*, *"au lieu de"*, etc.:

> *Pour* être jeune *, elle n'en est pas moins responsable.*
>
> concessive adverbial clause
> of *"n'est pas moins responsable"*
>
> For being so young, she's no less responsible.

● **a relative clause** in the indicative mood:

> *Lui* ‖ **qui d'habitude restait froid,** ‖ *s'enthousiasma.* (= *bien qu'il restât froid*)
>
> Usually he stays cool, but he got quite enthusiastic.

SUBORDINATE CONDITIONAL CLAUSES

A subordinate conditional adverbial clause indicates what condition is imposed by the action in the main clause. It answers the questions: *"à quelle condition?"*, "in what scenario?" *S'il n'avait pas couru si vite, il ne serait pas tombé./*If he hadn't run so fast, he wouldn't have fallen. *Il ne serait pas tombé à quelle condition? "S'il n'avait pas couru si vite"*: conjunctive subordinate clause, conditional complement of *"il ne serait pas tombé"*.

VARIOUS FORMS

Conjunctions	Moods	Examples
selon que, suivant que	indicative	*Selon que vous serez de son avis ou non,* ‖ *il vous estimera* ‖ *ou vous méprisera.* Whether or not you are of his opinion, he will either think well of you or disdain you.
à supposer que, pourvu que, à condition que, en admettant que, soit que... soit que, à moins que, pour peu que, que	subjunctive	*Elle doit tout ignorer encore de la nouvelle,* ‖ *à moins que vous n'ayez eu l'imprudence de la lui apprendre.* She must still be unaware of the news unless you were careless enough to tell her.
au cas où	conditional	*Au cas où elle accepterait,* ‖ *avertissez-moi.* In the case she accepts, let me know.
si	indicative	See following table

SUBORDINATE CONDITIONAL CLAUSES INTRODUCED BY "SI"

The subordinate conditional clause introduced by the conjunction *si* takes a verb in the indicative, but the tense varies with the meaning of the sentence and according to the mood and tense of the main clause.

NOTE : When a subordinate conditional clause is introduced by *si* and is followed by another subordinate conditional clause which is coordinated with it, this clause is introduced by *que* with its verb in the subjunctive:

*S'il vient **et que** je ne **sois** pas encore **arrivé**, faites-le attendre.* If he comes before I've arrived, ask him to wait.

Main clause	Subordinate clause with "si"	Examples
present indicative, imperfect, past historic and perfect, expressing a real event	indicative	*Si tu as quelque ennui, ‖ tu peux me le confier.* If you've any problems, you can tell me.
future indicative or imperative, expressing a future event	indicative present	*Si je l'apprends, ‖ je te le dirai.* If I hear about it, I'll tell you about it. *Si tu acceptes, téléphone-moi.* If you accept, phone me.
present conditional, expressing a possible future event	indicative imperfect	*Si je l'apprenais demain, ‖ je vous le dirais.* If I hear about it tomorrow, I'll tell you.
present conditional, expressing an impossible event at the present moment	indicative imperfect	*Si je le savais actuellement, ‖ je vous le dirais.* If I knew it now, I would tell you.
past conditional, expressing an event that could not have taken place in the past.	indicative pluperfect	*Si je l'avais su, ‖ je vous l'aurais dit.* If I had known it , I'd have told you.

OTHER CONDITIONAL EXPRESSIONS

The idea of condition can be expressed by:

● **a noun** as a conditional complement introduced by prepositions such as "sans", "avec", "selon", "sauf", "moyennant", "en cas de":

Sans votre appui ‖ il n'aurait pas réussi (= si vous ne lui aviez apporté…).
Without your support, he wouldn't have succeeded.

● **an infinitive** as a conditional complement introduced by the prepositions or prepositional phrases "à", "à condition de", "à moins de":

À lire ce roman, ‖ on croirait tous les hommes des scélérats. (= si on lit ce roman, on croit…)
Reading this novel, you'd believe that all men are villains.

● **a relative clause** in the conditional:

Celui ‖ qui te verrait désespérer ainsi ‖ douterait de ton courage. (= si on te voyait…)
Whoever would see you so desperate would doubt your courage.

SUBORDINATE COMPARATIVE CLAUSES

The subordinate comparative adverbial clause establishes a relationship of proportion, equality or inequality between itself and the main clause: *Je le retrouvais aussi souriant que je l'avais connu jadis.*/I found him as cheerful as I had known him in times past . *"que je l'avais connu jadis"* is a subordinate clause, adverbial phrase of comparison of *"Je le retrouvais aussi souriant"*.

VARIOUS FORMS

Conjunctions	Moods	Examples
Comparison: *de même que, ainsi que, tel que, comme*	indicative or conditional	*La famille en groupe allait se promener jusqu'à la jetée,* ǁ *ainsi qu'elle le faisait chaque dimanche.* The whole family walked as far as the jetty, just as they did each Sunday.
Equality or inequality: *aussi... que, autant... que; plus (moins)... que; autre... que*	indicative or conditional	*Lucie est aussi bavarde* ǁ *que son frère est taciturne.* Lucie is as talkative as her brother is taciturn. *Leur amitié fut courte, autant* ǁ *qu'elle était rare.* Their friendship was as brief as it was rare.
Proportion: *d'autant plus... que; dans la mesure... où; à mesure... que*	indicative	*Nous étions d'autant plus inquiets* ǁ *que le bois devenait maintenant plus épais.* We were all the more worried as the wood was now becoming thicker.

NOTE :

1. The subordinate comparative clauses are often not expressed by a verb; they are "elliptical": *Cela lui semblait lointain* ǁ *comme un mauvais rêve.*/To him it seemed far away, like a bad dream.

2. A subordinate clause starting with the conjunction *"comme si"* is called a comparative conditional: *Ses trois fils étaient vêtus tous de la même manière,* ǁ *comme s'ils avaient porté un uniforme.*/His three sons were all dressed in the same way, as if they were wearing a uniform.

OTHER COMPARATIVE EXPRESSIONS

The idea of comparison can also be expressed by the juxtaposing of two independent clauses: *Plus j'examinais les preuves retenues contre elle,* ǁ *plus je la croyais innocente.*/The more I looked at the proof held against her, the more I believed her innocent.; *Autant cet enfant est turbulent à la maison,* ǁ *autant il est sage en classe.*/This child is as disruptive at home, as he is well behaved in class.

SUBORDINATE PARTICIPIAL CLAUSES

A subordinate participial clause is formed by the present or past participle of which the subject expressed cannot be grammatically linked to any given word in the main clause.

TYPES OF SUBORDINATE PARTICIPIAL CLAUSES

A participial subordinate clause can be in the present or the past:

Le beau temps revenant, || *nous pourrons reprendre nos sorties.*/With the return of the good weather, we can resume our outings.: "*Le beau temps revenant*", participial clause formed from the present participle "*revenant*", where the subject "*beau temps*" is not linked to any word in the main clause.

⚠ On the contrary, there is no participial clause in the following example:

Ayant franchi la barrière, *nous nous sommes trouvés dans un jardin merveilleux.*/Having crossed the fence, we found ourselves in a marvellous garden.: the implied subject of "*ayant franchi*" is "*nous*", which is the actual subject of the main clause.

FUNCTIONS OF SUBORDINATE PARTICIPIAL CLAUSES

The subordinate participial clause can be an adverbial clause of:

– time:

Le silence rétabli, || *l'orateur prit la parole.*
Once silence was restored the orator took up his speech.

– cause:

La pluie ayant cessé, || *nous avons pu reprendre notre route.*
The rain having stopped, we were able to resume our way.

La fatigue venant, || *elle s'endormit.*
Tiredness coming on, she fell asleep.

– concession:

Ses erreurs cependant démontrées, || *il s'obstinait dans son opinion.*
Even though his errors were exposed he persisted in his opinion.

– condition:

Votre consentement une fois donné, || *nous pourrions aboutir.*
Once you've given your consent we should be able to come off.

AGREEMENT OF TENSE AND MOOD

The tense of the subordinate clause varies with the tense and mood of the main or subordinate clause on which it depends; this is what is called "tense agreement". This agreement can be determined by the meaning of the sentence, for example to express anteriority in relation to the tense in the main clause. It may also have no relationship with the meaning and yet be obligatory.

AGREEMENT WITH THE PRESENT TENSE

● When the main clause is in the present tense or the future indicative, the subordinate clause in the indicative can be in any tense, depending on the meaning:

Je crois
(present)
⟋ *qu'elle vient.* (today, now…): present
— *qu'elle est venue.* (yesterday, last year…): present perfect
⟍ *qu'elle viendra.* (tomorrow, next year…): future
} indicative

Il verra
(future)
⟋ *que j'ai raison.* (at this moment): present
⟍ *que j'avais raison.* (before, for a long time…): imperfect
} indicative

● When the main clause is in the present tense or the future indicative, the subordinate clause in the subjunctive is either in the present or the past:

Je crains
(present)
⟋ *qu'elle ne vienne.* (today…): present
⟍ *qu'elle ne soit venue.* (yesterday…): past
} subjunctive

Je n'admet-
trai pas
(future)
⟋ *qu'il s'absente.* (at this moment or later): present
⟍ *qu'il se soit absenté.* (before): past
} subjunctive

AGREEMENT WITH THE PAST TENSE

● When the main clause is in the past indicative or conditional, the subordinate clause in the indicative is either in the imperfect or the pluperfect. If it expresses the future it is the "future in the past" (formed by the present conditional):

Je croyais,
j'ai cru…
(past tense)
⟋ *qu'elle venait.* (simultaneity…): imperfect
— *qu'elle était venue.* (anteriority…): pluperfect
⟍ *qu'elle viendrait.* (posteriority…): present (conditionnal)
} indicative

170

● When the main clause is in a past indicative or conditional tense, the subordinate clause in the subjunctive is in the imperfect or pluperfect:

Je craignais, ⟋ *qu'il ne vînt.* (simultaneity): imperfect ⎫
J'avais craint... ⟍ *qu'il ne fût venu.* (anteriority): pluperfect ⎬ subjunctive
(past tense) ⎭

CASES OF NON-AGREEMENT

The rule of tense agreement is not observed:

– when the subordinate clause in the indicative or subjunctive has general validity:

*Il **savait** ‖ que toute vérité n'**est** pas bonne à dire.*

He knew that telling the whole truth can be dangerous.

*Il n'**admettait** pas ‖ que toute vérité ne **soit** bonne à dire.*

He wouldn't admit that telling the whole truth can be dangerous.

– when the subordinate clause in the subjunctive indicates an on-going action or something which is happening at the moment:

*J'**ai averti** ses amis ‖ afin qu'ils **fassent** la surprise.*

I warned his friends so that they could surprise him.

– when the subordinate clause in the subjunctive indicates a future action:

*J'**ai dit** ‖ qu'on m'**avertisse** dès qu'elle arrivera.*

I said that someone should warn me as soon as she arrived.

NOTE : Tense agreement is avoided in the 1st and 2nd person singular and the plural of the imperfect and pluperfect subjunctive, which is less and less used and is usually replaced by the present subjunctive.
In spoken language, the only use of the subjunctive is in the present and the past:

*Je regrette ‖ qu'il **soit** absent.* / I am sorry he is not there.
(today)   (today)

*J'ai regretté ‖ qu'il **soit** absent.* / I have been sorry he was not there.
(yesterday)   (yesterday)

*Je regrettais ‖ qu'il **soit** absent.* / I was sorry he was not there.
(yesterday)   (yesterday)

*J'ai regretté ‖ qu'il **ait été** absent.* / I have been sorry he had not
                                              been there.
(yesterday)   (before yesterday)

REPORTED SPEECH

There are several ways of reporting someone's comments or thoughts, according to whether are resorts or not to subordination and whether are uses or not a main verb of utterance (*dire, répondre, affirmer, exposer...*) or a verb of opinion (*croire, juger, penser, estimer...*).

DIRECT SPEECH

Direct speech consists in reporting the spoken words or thoughts of someone. The comments reported are placed between inverted commas and introduced by a strong punctuation mark; the clause which expresses the reported statement is not subordinated by a conjunction or an interrogative in the main clause:

> *Il dit: "Je me sens fatigué et je vais prendre quelques jours de vacances; j'irai me reposer en Bretagne, chez mes parents."*
> He said: "I feel tired and I'm going to take some time off; I'm going to my parents'in Brittany to have a rest."

INDIRECT SPEECH

Indirect speech consists in reporting the spoken words or thoughts of someone by making it dependent on the subordination of a verb of utterance or interrogation, then "introductory" verbs (e.g. *il dit que...*), by way of subordination. All the main and independent clauses in direct speech thus become subordinate clauses:

> *Il dit* ‖ *qu'il se sentait fatigué* ‖ *et qu'il allait prendre quelques jours de vacances;* ‖ *qu'il irait se reposer en Bretagne, chez ses parents.*
> He said that he felt tired and he was going to take some time off and would go to his parents' in Brittany to have a rest.

■ OTHER MODIFICATIONS

When passing from direct to indirect speech, there are a certain number of modifications in addition to subordination:

● **change of person** for personal and possessive pronouns:

> *il* or *elle* replaces *je; son* replaces *mon,* etc.;

● **change of mood** due to tense agreement:

– the present conditional, considered as "the future in the past", replaces the future indicative:

> direct speech: *"Je te prêterai ma voiture", dit-elle.*
> "I will lend you my car", she said.

indirect speech: *Elle m'a dit qu'elle me prêterait sa voiture.*
She told me she would lend me her car.

– in direct speech an order or interdiction is expressed by using the imperative or the subjunctive:

*On lui dit: "Ne vous **faites** pas de souci".*
They told him/her: "Don't worry".

In indirect speech, an order or interdiction is expressed by using the subjunctive:

*On lui dit qu'elle ne se **fasse** pas de souci.*
They told her she shouldn't worry.

● **changes in the temporal or spatial criterion:** *maintenant* becomes *alors; hier* becomes *la veille; ici* becomes *là,* etc.:

*Il lui dit: "Je suis **maintenant** trop occupé, mais je vous recevrai **ici** demain."* (direct speech)/He told her: "I'm too busy at the moment, but I will see you here tomorrow." → *Il lui dit qu'il était **alors** (or **pour le moment**) trop occupé, mais qu'il la recevrai **là le lendemain**.* (indirect speech)/He told him he was too busy for the moment but he would see him there the next day.

INTERROGATION IN INDIRECT SPEECH

● Interrogative words are the same in direct and indirect interrogation, except for *"est-ce que"*, which becomes *"si"*, and *"qu'est-ce qui"*, which becomes *"ce qui"*, *"ce que"*:

"Est-ce que vous me comprenez ?" → *Elle lui a demandé **s'**il la comprenait.*
"Do you understand me?" → she asked him if he understood her.

"Qu'est-ce qui se passe ?" → *Je me demande **ce qui** se passe.*
"What's happening ?" → I wonder what's happening.

Inversion of the subject of direct interrogation generally does not take place in indirect interrogation:

Je vous le demande: "Où irez-vous ?" → *Je vous demande où **vous irez**.*
I ask you: "Where are you going ?" → I ask you where you are going.

However, inversion is possible if the subject of the interrogative is not a personal pronoun and if the interrogative word is not *"pourquoi"*:

Je vous le demande: "Où vont tous ces gens ?" → *Je vous demande où vont tous ces gens.*

I ask you: "where are all these people going?" → I ask you where all these people are going.

173

FREE INDIRECT SPEECH

Free indirect speech consists in getting rid of the main introductory clause (e.g. *il dit que...*), while, at the same time, keeping the person, the tense, the mood and the time and place adverbs of indirect speech:

> *Il se sentait fatigué et il allait prendre quelques jours de vacances; il irait se reposer en Bretagne, chez ses parents.*

NOTE : The imperfect is the tense most often used in free indirect speech; but the pluperfect and conditional can also be found (in the sense of the "future in the past").

> *Il rassura tout le monde: il n'**avait** pas **été** sérieusement malade, et il **serait** bientôt rétabli.*

> He reassured everybody: he had not been seriously ill, and would soon be better.

REGISTER

Register is how an individual uses the consituent elements of a language (vocabulary, morphology, syntax, phonetics). If the study of register does not fall within a systematic exposure of a language, it must, nevertheless, be supported by general principles and usual procedures.

LEVELS OF LANGUAGE

Several levels of language can be distinguished in French.
A letter is not written in the same way as a piece of work for publication or for an official speech. A friend is not addressed in the same way as a superior. The same language is not heard in the street, a building site or a school yard as is heard in the art gallery or during a university lecture. Different language is used with people of different status or age. There is a written language and a spoken language. Each of the above is characterised by the use of words or constructions corresponding to what is called "the level of language":

– spoken language can be familiar, popular or slang;
– written language can be everyday, administrative, formal or literary.

LEXIS

● Certain synonyms belong to different levels of language:

trépas/demise (literary) and *mort*/death (everyday); *ouvrage*/work (formal) and *livre*/book (everyday):

camarade/friend (everyday) and *copain*/mate (familiar); *convier* (formal) and *inviter*/to invite (everyday);

courroux/wrath (literary) and *colère*/anger (everyday); *vêtir*/to clothe (formal) and *habiller*/to dress (everyday).

● Writing in formal register:

Des bruits infamants se répandaient, mettant en cause sa réputation.
Injurious rumours were spreading, questioning his reputation.

Spoken register:

Les voisins n'arrêtaient pas de déblatérer sur son compte.
The neighbours never stop ranting on about him.

MORPHOLOGY

● Usually, written language is in the past historic.
In spoken language the past historic has been replaced by the perfect tense.

● The semi-auxiliary *"aller"* is more often used in spoken language than in written one to express the future.

● Spoken language often avoids verbs of the third conjugation and replaces them with verbs from the first conjugation:

émouvoir is replaced by *émotionner;*
résoudre is replaced by *solutionner.*

■SYNTAX

● Written language is more likely to be translated by the subordinating logical relationship which in spoken language is readily expressed by coordination or simple juxtaposition.
So, in written language:

Comme il pleut encore, les inondations vont s'aggraver.
As it is still raining, the floods are going to get worse.

Il pleut tellement que les inondations vont s'aggraver.
It's raining so much that the floods are going to get worse.

But in spoken language:

Il pleut toujours: les inondations vont s'aggraver.
It's still raining; the floods are going to get worse.

● Written language uses the subjunctive after verbs expressing negative thoughts:

Je ne pense pas qu'il vienne.
I don't think he is coming.

Spoken language uses the indicative:

Je ne pense pas qu'il viendra.

NOTE : To judge an author's register, look at the kind of language used, which will vary according to the type of literary register adopted or the person who is speaking. In one piece of literary work, the same writer can use several levels of language.

TECHNICAL AND SCIENTIFIC LANGUAGES

Besides usual language, written or spoken, each professional group uses a specialized language: doctors, teachers, computer scientists, advertisers, metallurgists, chemists, all have their own vocabulary.
The world of science and technology creates its own words. These words are not necessarily understood by those who do not belong to that profession or have not studied that particular science:

– in surgery, they talk about *"appendicectomie"* whereas the layman only understands that it is an operation for appendicitis;

– in printing, all the characters used have the same name for the layman (they are letters), but the technical expert distinguishes between *"plantin"* and *"garamond"*;

– in the field of agriculture, everyone knows about the tractor, but only the technical expert knows what a *"tambour de dégagement"* /rear-beater is.

The advantage of technical words is that they are precise, relating as they do to one sole object or operation.

ARCHAISMS AND NEOLOGISMS

The French language has evolved a lot since the Middle Ages; words and expressions have changed in meaning, become outdated or simply disappeared, whilst others have appeared.

The use of a word from a previous age is called an "archaism":

inclination for *"amour"*, *aéroplane* for *"avion"*.

The use of a word recently introduced into a language is called a "neologism":

cibler, câblodistribution, logiciel, fast-food, scénariser, bioéthique.

TECHNIQUES IN REGISTER

The techniques or the effects of register bring different aspects of language into play and allow ideas or feelings to be expressed in a more personal way.

▓ IMAGE, COMPARISON & METAPHOR

Image is created by the comparison of two objects very close to each other because of an analogy of shape, colour or weight, etc. So you say, *"une feuille de papier"* by comparison with *"la feuille d'un arbre"*.

This is a technique in register which can take two forms:

– comparative, with the use of *"comme"*, *"ainsi que"*, *"de même"*, etc.:

*Quand le ciel bas et lourd pèse **comme** un couvercle...* (Baudelaire)

– metaphoric, without a comparative word:

*Les choses qui **chantent** dans la tête...* (Verlaine)

▓ TRANSPOSITION

This consists in transferring a word from its normal field to a closely associated field. So you will say:

– *une odeur **grasse**/*a greasy smell, by analogy with the sense of touch;
– *un texte **opaque**/*an opaque text, by analogy with sight.

▓ TRANSFER OF MEANING AND METONYMY

This is the transfer of a meaning to a word from another given word which resembles it in form. So *fruste*, which originally signified *"usé"/worn out*, has taken on the meaning of *"grossier"/crude, uncouth*, because of its closeness to *rustre*/peasant, boor. In metonymy, this link can represent the whole part, transferring from a constituent part to the whole:

> *Une voile à l'horizon, c'est un navire.*
> (*la voile*/a sail, part of the ship, indicates the whole ship).

PARAPHRASING

Paraphrasing consists in replacing a precise word by its definition, in order to avoid a monotonous repetition of the same term or to add a memorable idea to a simple word.
In saying *"Le fondateur de Québec est mort en 1635."* instead *of "Samuel de Champlain est mort en 1635."*, the emphasis is on his role in Canadian history and not on his very general qualities as a French explorer.

VARIETY

This consists in replacing a word by its synonym, in order to avoid repetition. As no word is absolutely synonymous with another, the synonymy can be intended to give more weight to the expression, more abundance (through redundancy), or to be more precise about the first term by using a series of equivalents:

> *Nos interprétations trop fines et subtiles.*(Saint-Beuve)
> Our interpretations too keen and subtle

> *C'est le courbement, la courbure, la courbature, l'inclinaison de l'écrivain sur sa table de travail.* (Ch. Péguy)
> *This is the curving, the curvature, the painful bending of the writer on his working table.*

ACCUMULATION

Accumulation consists in enumeration where the whole can be summed up in a single word and where the effect is to give the idea of greatness or force:

> *Déroute: enfants, vieillards, bœufs, moutons; clameur vaine* (Victor Hugo)

INVERSION

Inversion consists in presenting words in an order which is not usual in common language:

> *La chambre est pleine d'ombre; on entend vaguement*

> **De deux enfants** *le triste et doux chuchotement* (Arthur Rimbaud)

This technique is found particularly in poetry.

VERSIFICATION

| Versification is all the phonetic and rhythmic rules which govern the art of writing in verse. | It is a technique which, by itself, is not sufficient to create poetic text. |

FRENCH VERSE

Traditional French verse has three essential characteristics:

– it is made up of a certain fixed number of syllables; this is the verse metre;

– it finishes with a rhyme, repeating the same sound at the end of two lines of verse;

– it has a certain rhythm characterised by one or several pauses (cuts), accentuated syllables and certain sonorities:

*Nous partîmes cinq **cents**; ‖ mais par un **prompt** renfort*

*Nous nous **vîmes** trois **mille** ‖ en arrivant au port (Corneille)*

verse of 12 syllables; rhyming words *ren-fort, p-ort;* pause in the middle of each line; rhythmic stress on the 3rd, 6th, 10th, and 12th syllables.

VERSE METRE

▨ NUMBER OF SYLLABLES

– 12 syllables (alexandrine):

Quand ils eurent fini de clore et de murer,
On mit l'aïeul au centre en une tour de pierre (Victor Hugo)

– 10 syllables (decasyllabic):

Ce toit tranquille, où marchent les colombes
Entre les pins palpite, entre les tombes (Paul Valéry)

– 8 syllables (octosyllabic):

Comme le cygne allait nageant
Sur le lac au miroir d'argent (Théodore de Banville)

– 7 syllables:

Quand les blés sont sous la grêle
Fou qui fait le délicat (Louis Aragon)

– 6 syllables:

De la rose charmante à l'ombre de rosier
Si mollement ouverte (Anna de Noailles)

– 3 or 2 syllables:

> ***Sauve-moi***
> *Joue avec moi*
> ***Oiseau*** (Jacques Prévert)

Generally, all the syllables in a word count. But there are some particular cases:

● Rule for mute **-e**:

– preceded by a consonant and followed by another one (or an aspirated **h**), it counts as a syllable, except at the end of the line:

> *Et **le** soir on lançait de flè**ches** aux étoiles* (Victo Hugo)

– preceded by a vowel or a consonant and before a vowel (or a mute **h**), it is elided and is not counted:

> *Notre profond silenc**e a**busant leurs esprits* (Corneille)

– preceded by a vowel inside a word, it is not counted:

> *Après, je châti**er**ai les railleurs, s'il en reste* (Victor Hugo)

● **-ent,** plural verb ending, preceded by a vowel is not counted:

> *Tous ses fils regarda**ient** trembler l'aïeul farouche* (Victor Hugo)

● The vowel group **-ion, -ier, -iez** generally count as one syllable, but usage is variable:

> *La Ré-vo-lu-**ti-on** leur cri-ait: "Vo-lon-taires…"* (Victor Hugo)
>
> *Et les pieds sans sou-liers* (Victor Hugo)

When two vowels meet and the first is not elided, there is a hiatus. The hiatus was avoided in the poetry of the XVIIth and XVIIIth centuries, but has been present since then:

> *Et, durant tout un jour, j'**ai eu** toute Venise* (Henri de Régnier)

RHYME

The repetition of the same sound at the end of two lines of verse is called "rhyme"; this sound is a vowel, supported or not by several consonants:

> *oubl-**i**, ennem-**i**; armi-**stice**, ju-**stice***

The rhyming words can have different spelling:

> *accomp-**li**, dé-**lit***

● Nature of rhyme:

– masculine (not finishing in a mute **-e**):

> *Soudain, comme chacun demeurait inter**dit**,*
> *Un jeune homme bien fait sortit des rangs, et **dit**…* (Victor Hugo)

– feminine (ending in a mute **-e**):

L'empereur, souriant, reprit d'un air tranquille:
— Duc, tu ne m'a pas dit le nom de cette ville? (Victor Hugo)

NOTE : Alexandrines ending with a feminine rhyming word would have 13 syllables if the last one is was pronounced clearly.

In the great classical works in alexandrines, the practice is to alternate the masculine and feminine rhyming words.

● Rhyming quality:

– imperfect (only vowels): *destinée, veillée...;*
– adequate (vowel + consonant or consonant + vowel): *destinée, année*:
– perfect (vowel + consonant + vowel or consonant + vowel + consonant, or maybe longer): *destinée, matinée.*

● Rhyming arrangement:

– couplets:	a *Il est ainsi de pauvres cœurs*
	a *Avec, en eux, des lacs de pleurs,*
	b *Qui sont pâles comme les pierres*
	b *D'un cimetière* (Emile Verhaeren)
– alternate:	a *Depuis six mille ans la guerre*
	b *Plaît aux hommes querelleurs*
	a *Et Dieu perd son temps à faire*
	b *Les étoiles et les fleurs* (Victor Hugo)
– abba rhyme sheme:	a *Le soir ramène le silence*
	b *Assis sur ces rochers déserts*
	b *Je suis dans le vague des airs*
	a *Le char de la nuit qui s'avance* (Alphonse de Lamartine)

RYTHM

● **The cut**. Within a line of verse, there are one or several pauses, called "cuts".
The cut in the alexandrine generally happens after the 6th syllable (caesura); it cuts the line into two equal parts (hemistich):

Heureux ceux qui sont morts ‖ pour la terre charnelle

Mais pourvu que ce fût ‖ dans une juste guerre (Charles Péguy)

Sometimes, in romantic poetry, the alexandrine is divided into three parts by two cuts:

Pluie ou bourrasque, ‖ il faut qu'il sorte, ‖ il faut qu'il aille (Victor Hugo)

NOTE : Octosyllabic verse is usually cut after the 3rd or 4th syllable, decasyllabic verse after the 4th.

● **Enjambment and rejet.** When the end of a line of verse does not coincide with a possible pause in normal delivery, enjambement occurs and the part of the phrase moved to the beginning of the following line is called the "rejet":

> *Jubal, père de ceux qui passent dans les bourgs*
> *Soufflant dans les clairons et frappant des tambours,*
> **Cria**: *Je saurai bien construire une barrière (Victor Hugo)*

"*Cria*" is a rejet.

● **Rhythmic stress.** There are several stressed syllables in a line of verse; their position, which is variable, and the nature of the stressed syllables all come together to form the music of the verse:

> *De la rumeur humaine et du monde oublieux,*
> *Il regarde le mer, les bois et les collines* (Leconte de Lisle)

POETRY

A poem is made up of a string of lines; these lines can be grouped into stanzas, each stanza presenting a complete meaning and having its own rhythm.

● Stanzas are a group of lines; each having a precise name according to the number of lines involved:

2 lines: *distique*	5 lines: *quintain*	8 lines: *huitain*
3 lines: *tercet*	6 lines: *sizain*	9 lines: *neuvain*
4 lines: *quatrain*	7 lines: *septain*	10 lines: *dizain*

● Poetry in a set form has a determinate structure: number of lines, stanzas, rhyme scheme, etc.
A sonnet is thus composed of 14 lines split into 2 quatrains (2 rhymes) and 2 tercets (3 rhymes):

Comme le champ semé en verdure foisonne,	1st quatrain; rhyming:	a
De verdure se hausse en tuyau verdissant,		b
De tuyau se hérisse en épi florissant,		b
D'épi jaunit en grain que le chaud assaisonne;		a

Et comme en la saison le rustique moissonne	2nd quatrain; rhyming:	a
Les ondoyants cheveux du sillon blondissant,		b
Les met d'ordre en javelle, et du blé jaunissant		b
Sur le champ dépouillé mille gerbes façonne:		a

Ainsi de peu à peu crût l'Empire romain,	1st tercet; rhyming:	c
Tant qu'il fut dépouillé par la barbare main,		c
Qui ne laissa de lui que ces marques antiques,		d

Que chacun va pillant: comme on voit le glaneur,	2nd tercet; rhyming:	e
Cheminant pas à pas, recueillir les reliques		d
De ce qui va tombant après le moissonneur.		e

Joachim du Bellay

NOTE : The ballad and rondeau are also a set form of poetry.

APPENDICE

PRONUNCIATION AND WORD SPELLING

Phonetics studies the nature of sounds, their development and their distribution within a given language. As in English, spelling in French does not match pronunciation consistently, and one needs to distinguish between the two.

PRONUNCIATION AND SPELLING

Sounds (phonetic symbols)		Examples	Letters (spelling)
[a]	-a- short front vowel	*lac, cave, agate, béat, maille, soi, moelle, moyen, il plongea*	a, (e)a, a(i), oi, oy, œ (= oua)
[ɑ]	-a- long back vowel	*case, fable, sabre, flamme, âme, douceâtre, tas*	a, â, (e)â
[e]	-é- closed high	*année, pays, désobéir, œdème, je mangeai*	é, ay, e(i), eai, ai, œ
[ɛ]	-è- open	*bec, poète, blême, Noël, il peigne, il aime, fraîche, j'aimais*	è, ê, e, ë, ei, ai, aî
[i]	-i- short or long	*île, mille, épître, tu lis, partir, cyprès, dîner, naïf*	i, î, y, ï
[ɔ]	-o- open short or long	*note, robe, mode, col, roche, Paul, port*	o, au
[o]	-o- closed short or long	*coaguler, drôle, aube, agneau, sot, pôle, mot, geôle*	o, ô, au, eau, (e)ô
[u]	-ou-	*outil, mou, pour, joue, goût, août*	ou(e), oû, aoû
[y]	-u-	*usage, luth, mur, uni, sûr, il eut, vue, déçu*	u, û, eu, u(e)
[œ]	-eu- open short or long	*peuple, bœuf, chevreuil, œil, jeune, douceur*	eu, œu, eu(i), œ(i)
[ø]	-eu- closed short or long	*émeute, jeûne, aveu, nœud, eux, bleu*	eu, eû, œu
[ə]	-e-	*me, remède, grelotter, vous seriez*	e
[ɛ̄]	-è- nasalisé ouvert	*timbre, matin, impie, main, bien, faim, dessein, lymphe, syncope*	im, in, en, aim, ain, ein, ym, yn
[ɑ̄]	-a- nasalisé	*champ, ange, emballer, ennui, vengeance, taon, paon*	am, an, em, en, ean, aon

Sounds (phonetic symbols)		Examples	Letters (spelling)
[ɔ̃]	-o- nasalisé	*plomb, ongle, mon, uncial*	on, om, un
[œ̃]	-eu- nasalisé	*parfum, aucun, brun, à jeun*	un, um, eun
[j]	-y (e)-	*yeux, lieu, fermier, liasse, piller, pied, bien*	y, i, ll (after -i- and + vowel)
[ɥ]	-u (i, e, a, etc.)-	*lui, nuit, suivre, huit, enduit, huer*	u (+ vowel)
[w]	-ou (i, e, a, etc.)-	*oui, ouest, moi, squale, louer*	ou (+ vowel) oi (= oua), u (a)
[p]	-pe-	*prendre, apporter, stop, loupe*	p, pp
[b]	-be-	*bateau, combler, aborder, abbé, snob*	b, bb
[d]	-de-	*dalle, addition, cadenas, raide, lad*	d, dd
[t]	-te-	*train, théâtre, vendetta, rite, kit*	t, th, tt
[k]	-ke-	*coq, quatre, carte, képi, kilo, squelette, lac, accabler, bacchante, chrome, chlore, chœur, choléra*	q, c (+ a, o, u), k, qu, c, cc, cch, ch (+ r, l), ch
[g]	-gue-	*guêpe, dague, diagnostic, garder, gondole, goulag*	g (+ a, o), gu, gn, g
[f]	-fe-	*fable, physique, fez, chef, neuf*	f, ph
[v]	-ve-	*voir, wagon, aviver, révolte, rive*	v, w
[s]	-se-	*savant, science, tasse, cela, ciel, façon, ça, reçu, patience, façade, muscle*	s, sc, ss, c (+ e, i), ç (+ a, o, u), t (i)
[z]	-ze-	*zèle, azur, réseau, rasade, rasoir*	z, s (between vowels)
[ʒ]	-je-	*jabot, déjouer, jongleur, âgé, germe, gigot*	j, g (+ i, e)
[ʃ]	-che-	*charrue, échec, schéma, shah, moche*	ch, sch, sh
[l]	-le-	*lier, bal, intelligence, illettré, calcul*	l, ll
[m]	-me-	*amas, mât, drame, grammaire*	m, mm
[n]	-ne-	*nager, naine, neuf, animal, dictionnaire*	n, nn
[r]	-re-	*rare, arracher, âpre, sabre, tenir*	r, rr
[ɲ]	-gne-	*agneau, peigner, baigner, besogne*	gn

NOTES :
1. Exceptions are not included in this table; it should be remembered that the same spelling sometimes has different pronunciations. Only usage and a good dictionary can indicate the most current pronunciation in cases of difficulty.
2. The letter **-x-** has two pronunciations [ks] or [gz]: *axe* but *exemple*.
3. The letter **-h-** is not pronounced and is not aspirated. What is called the aspirated **-h-** prevents linking from occuring.

WORD LINKING

● Certain final consonants are not pronounced when the word is isolated:

avant [avɑ̃]   trop [tro]   *nous sommes* [nusɔm]   but

Il est arrivé avant elle. [avɑ̃tɛl]   *Ces souliers sont trop étroits.* [tropetrwa]

⚠ Sometimes consonants change their pronunciation: **-d** is pronounced like **-t**, **-g** is pronounced like **-k**, **-s** and **-x** are pronounced like **-z**:

Nous nous sommes ennuyés. [nusɔmzɑ̃ nɥije]

Elle m'a fourni un grand appui. [grɑ̃ tapɥi]

● Linking occurs naturally when the consonant is pronounced in the separated word: *Elle doit partir en voyage.* [partirɑ̃ vwajaz]

● In general, linking occurs between words linked by meaning and which form a group. Thus, there is always linking between:

– a verb and a subject pronoun: *Ils ont perdu.; On a oublié.*

– a verb and a noun or an attributive adjective: *Il est heureux.; Ils sont étudiants.*

– a verb and a direct object infinitive: *Il veut aller à Winnipeg.;*

– a verb and its auxiliary: *Tu es émue.; Nous avons attrapé la balle.;*

– a noun and an article: *les enfants; les hommes;*

– a noun and an epithet adjective or a pronoun: *mes autres amies; les bons amis;*

– a preposition and its group (the noun or the pronoun that it introduces), except **hors**, **selon**, **vers**, **envers**: *Cela s'est passé sans incident.;*

– an adverb and the word it modifies: *tout entier;*

– **c'est**, **quand**, **dont** and the word following: *le livre dont il me parle; quand il vient; C'est à vous que je le conseille.*

● Linking occurs between ready-made sayings and expressions:

de plus en plus; mot à mot.

185

● Linking never occurs:

– after an **-s** in compound words: *des arcs-en-ciel* [ark ɑ̃ sjɛl];

– after the final unpronounced consonant of a singular noun and the following epithet adjective: *un poing ‖ énorme;*

– after the conjunction **et**: *Et ‖ elle m'a dit de venir.*

NOTE : Linking is often optional. The tendency in everyday language is currently to limit it as far as possible; in the theatre and in public speaking, on the other hand, linking is maintained. Frequently, there are two possibilities: *Il va droit au but.* or *Il va droit au͜ but.*

SPELLING MARKS

● **Accents**. French has three accents: the acute accent, the grave accent, and the circumflex accent:

– the **acute** accent indicates a closed **-e-** (except before final **-d, -z-, -f-, -r-,** or where **-e-** is written without accent):

  beauté; solidité; fée; ému; but *pied; fermer; nez; fief;*

– the **grave** accent indicates an open **-e-;** when put over **-a-** and **-u-** it distinguishes between homonyms:

  mère; décès; il mène; là distinguished from *la; ou* from *où, à* from *a;*

– the **circumflex** accent indicates a vowel whose pronunciation is lengthened through the disappearence of a former consonant (**-s-**) or a vowel (**-e-**):

  bâtir (from the Old French *bastir*); *château* (from *chasteau*); *sûr* (from *seur*).

● The **dieresis** (¨) is placed over **-e-, -i-, -u-** in order to indicate that one of the vowels is detached by pronunciation from the preceding one: *aiguë* is pronounced [gy] and not [gə]; *Saül* [sayl]; *haïr* [air].

● The **cedilla** accent, which is placed under **-c-** (**-ç-**) before **-a-, -o-, -u-,** indicates that the **-c-** is pronounced [s]: *façon; reçu; nous plaçons; il plaçait.*

● The **apostrophe** marks the elision of a vowel with the initial vowel of a word that follows (which can be preceded by a silent **-h-**):

  j'apprends; l'aurore; jusqu'à minuit; je t'aide; l'horloge.

● The **hyphen** is placed between each element of a compound word:

  arc-en-ciel; garde-fou; va-et-vient.

It is also placed between a verb and a reversed subject pronoun:

  Venez-vous? Avez-vous vu? A-t-elle mangé?

⚠ Some compound words do not have a hyphen: *pomme de terre; poids lourd.*

ALPHABETICAL INDEX

Imprimé en Italie par Rotolito LOMBARDA
Dépôt légal 1ʳᵉ édition : décembre 2001
Dépôt légal : mai 2002
N° de projet : 10096246 (II) 7 (OSB 90°)